C-3572   CAREER EXAMINATION SERIES

This is your
PASSBOOK for...

Clerk-Typist II

Test Preparation Study Guide
Questions & Answers

COPYRIGHT NOTICE

This book is SOLELY intended for, is sold ONLY to, and its use is RESTRICTED to individual, bona fide applicants or candidates who qualify by virtue of having seriously filed applications for appropriate license, certificate, professional and/or promotional advancement, higher school matriculation, scholarship, or other legitimate requirements of education and/or governmental authorities.

This book is NOT intended for use, class instruction, tutoring, training, duplication, copying, reprinting, excerption, or adaptation, etc., by:

1) Other publishers
2) Proprietors and/or Instructors of "Coaching" and/or Preparatory Courses
3) Personnel and/or Training Divisions of commercial, industrial, and governmental organizations
4) Schools, colleges, or universities and/or their departments and staffs, including teachers and other personnel
5) Testing Agencies or Bureaus
6) Study groups which seek by the purchase of a single volume to copy and/or duplicate and/or adapt this material for use by the group as a whole without having purchased individual volumes for each of the members of the group
7) Et al.

Such persons would be in violation of appropriate Federal and State statutes.

PROVISION OF LICENSING AGREEMENTS – Recognized educational, commercial, industrial, and governmental institutions and organizations, and others legitimately engaged in educational pursuits, including training, testing, and measurement activities, may address request for a licensing agreement to the copyright owners, who will determine whether, and under what conditions, including fees and charges, the materials in this book may be used them. In other words, a licensing facility exists for the legitimate use of the material in this book on other than an individual basis. However, it is asseverated and affirmed here that the material in this book CANNOT be used without the receipt of the express permission of such a licensing agreement from the Publishers. Inquiries re licensing should be addressed to the company, attention rights and permissions department.

All rights reserved, including the right of reproduction in whole or in part, in any form or by any means, electronic or mechanical, including photocopying, recording, or by any information storage and retrieval system, without permission in writing from the Publisher.

Copyright © 2024 by
National Learning Corporation

212 Michael Drive, Syosset, NY 11791
(516) 921-8888 • www.passbooks.com
E-mail: info@passbooks.com

PUBLISHED IN THE UNITED STATES OF AMERICA

PASSBOOK® SERIES

THE *PASSBOOK® SERIES* has been created to prepare applicants and candidates for the ultimate academic battlefield – the examination room.

At some time in our lives, each and every one of us may be required to take an examination – for validation, matriculation, admission, qualification, registration, certification, or licensure.

Based on the assumption that every applicant or candidate has met the basic formal educational standards, has taken the required number of courses, and read the necessary texts, the *PASSBOOK® SERIES* furnishes the one special preparation which may assure passing with confidence, instead of failing with insecurity. Examination questions – together with answers – are furnished as the basic vehicle for study so that the mysteries of the examination and its compounding difficulties may be eliminated or diminished by a sure method.

This book is meant to help you pass your examination provided that you qualify and are serious in your objective.

The entire field is reviewed through the huge store of content information which is succinctly presented through a provocative and challenging approach – the question-and-answer method.

A climate of success is established by furnishing the correct answers at the end of each test.

You soon learn to recognize types of questions, forms of questions, and patterns of questioning. You may even begin to anticipate expected outcomes.

You perceive that many questions are repeated or adapted so that you can gain acute insights, which may enable you to score many sure points.

You learn how to confront new questions, or types of questions, and to attack them confidently and work out the correct answers.

You note objectives and emphases, and recognize pitfalls and dangers, so that you may make positive educational adjustments.

Moreover, you are kept fully informed in relation to new concepts, methods, practices, and directions in the field.

You discover that you are actually taking the examination all the time: you are preparing for the examination by "taking" an examination, not by reading extraneous and/or supererogatory textbooks.

In short, this PASSBOOK®, used directedly, should be an important factor in helping you to pass your test.

CLERK TYPIST II

DUTIES

Performs varied typing and clerical work; may assign and instruct a staff of subordinate clerical personnel; performs related duties as required.

SCOPE OF EXAMINATION

Written test will cover knowledge, skills, and/or abilities in such areas as:
1. Spelling;
2. English grammar and usage, punctuation;
3. Keyboarding practices;
4. Office record keeping;
5. Office practices;
6. Alphabetizing; and
7. Arithmetic.

HOW TO TAKE A TEST

I. YOU MUST PASS AN EXAMINATION

A. *WHAT EVERY CANDIDATE SHOULD KNOW*

Examination applicants often ask us for help in preparing for the written test. What can I study in advance? What kinds of questions will be asked? How will the test be given? How will the papers be graded?

As an applicant for a civil service examination, you may be wondering about some of these things. Our purpose here is to suggest effective methods of advance study and to describe civil service examinations.

Your chances for success on this examination can be increased if you know how to prepare. Those "pre-examination jitters" can be reduced if you know what to expect. You can even experience an adventure in good citizenship if you know why civil service exams are given.

B. *WHY ARE CIVIL SERVICE EXAMINATIONS GIVEN?*

Civil service examinations are important to you in two ways. As a citizen, you want public jobs filled by employees who know how to do their work. As a job seeker, you want a fair chance to compete for that job on an equal footing with other candidates. The best-known means of accomplishing this two-fold goal is the competitive examination.

Exams are widely publicized throughout the nation. They may be administered for jobs in federal, state, city, municipal, town or village governments or agencies.

Any citizen may apply, with some limitations, such as the age or residence of applicants. Your experience and education may be reviewed to see whether you meet the requirements for the particular examination. When these requirements exist, they are reasonable and applied consistently to all applicants. Thus, a competitive examination may cause you some uneasiness now, but it is your privilege and safeguard.

C. *HOW ARE CIVIL SERVICE EXAMS DEVELOPED?*

Examinations are carefully written by trained technicians who are specialists in the field known as "psychological measurement," in consultation with recognized authorities in the field of work that the test will cover. These experts recommend the subject matter areas or skills to be tested; only those knowledges or skills important to your success on the job are included. The most reliable books and source materials available are used as references. Together, the experts and technicians judge the difficulty level of the questions.

Test technicians know how to phrase questions so that the problem is clearly stated. Their ethics do not permit "trick" or "catch" questions. Questions may have been tried out on sample groups, or subjected to statistical analysis, to determine their usefulness.

Written tests are often used in combination with performance tests, ratings of training and experience, and oral interviews. All of these measures combine to form the best-known means of finding the right person for the right job.

II. HOW TO PASS THE WRITTEN TEST

A. NATURE OF THE EXAMINATION

To prepare intelligently for civil service examinations, you should know how they differ from school examinations you have taken. In school you were assigned certain definite pages to read or subjects to cover. The examination questions were quite detailed and usually emphasized memory. Civil service exams, on the other hand, try to discover your present ability to perform the duties of a position, plus your potentiality to learn these duties. In other words, a civil service exam attempts to predict how successful you will be. Questions cover such a broad area that they cannot be as minute and detailed as school exam questions.

In the public service similar kinds of work, or positions, are grouped together in one "class." This process is known as *position-classification*. All the positions in a class are paid according to the salary range for that class. One class title covers all of these positions, and they are all tested by the same examination.

B. FOUR BASIC STEPS

1) Study the announcement

How, then, can you know what subjects to study? Our best answer is: "Learn as much as possible about the class of positions for which you've applied." The exam will test the knowledge, skills and abilities needed to do the work.

Your most valuable source of information about the position you want is the official exam announcement. This announcement lists the training and experience qualifications. Check these standards and apply only if you come reasonably close to meeting them.

The brief description of the position in the examination announcement offers some clues to the subjects which will be tested. Think about the job itself. Review the duties in your mind. Can you perform them, or are there some in which you are rusty? Fill in the blank spots in your preparation.

Many jurisdictions preview the written test in the exam announcement by including a section called "Knowledge and Abilities Required," "Scope of the Examination," or some similar heading. Here you will find out specifically what fields will be tested.

2) Review your own background

Once you learn in general what the position is all about, and what you need to know to do the work, ask yourself which subjects you already know fairly well and which need improvement. You may wonder whether to concentrate on improving your strong areas or on building some background in your fields of weakness. When the announcement has specified "some knowledge" or "considerable knowledge," or has used adjectives like "beginning principles of..." or "advanced ... methods," you can get a clue as to the number and difficulty of questions to be asked in any given field. More questions, and hence broader coverage, would be included for those subjects which are more important in the work. Now weigh your strengths and weaknesses against the job requirements and prepare accordingly.

3) Determine the level of the position

Another way to tell how intensively you should prepare is to understand the level of the job for which you are applying. Is it the entering level? In other words, is this the position in which beginners in a field of work are hired? Or is it an intermediate or advanced level? Sometimes this is indicated by such words as "Junior" or "Senior" in the class title. Other jurisdictions use Roman numerals to designate the level – Clerk I, Clerk II, for example. The word "Supervisor" sometimes appears in the title. If the level is not indicated by the title, check the description of duties. Will you be working under very close supervision, or will you have responsibility for independent decisions in this work?

4) Choose appropriate study materials

Now that you know the subjects to be examined and the relative amount of each subject to be covered, you can choose suitable study materials. For beginning level jobs, or even advanced ones, if you have a pronounced weakness in some aspect of your training, read a modern, standard textbook in that field. Be sure it is up to date and has general coverage. Such books are normally available at your library, and the librarian will be glad to help you locate one. For entry-level positions, questions of appropriate difficulty are chosen -- neither highly advanced questions, nor those too simple. Such questions require careful thought but not advanced training.

If the position for which you are applying is technical or advanced, you will read more advanced, specialized material. If you are already familiar with the basic principles of your field, elementary textbooks would waste your time. Concentrate on advanced textbooks and technical periodicals. Think through the concepts and review difficult problems in your field.

These are all general sources. You can get more ideas on your own initiative, following these leads. For example, training manuals and publications of the government agency which employs workers in your field can be useful, particularly for technical and professional positions. A letter or visit to the government department involved may result in more specific study suggestions, and certainly will provide you with a more definite idea of the exact nature of the position you are seeking.

III. KINDS OF TESTS

Tests are used for purposes other than measuring knowledge and ability to perform specified duties. For some positions, it is equally important to test ability to make adjustments to new situations or to profit from training. In others, basic mental abilities not dependent on information are essential. Questions which test these things may not appear as pertinent to the duties of the position as those which test for knowledge and information. Yet they are often highly important parts of a fair examination. For very general questions, it is almost impossible to help you direct your study efforts. What we can do is to point out some of the more common of these general abilities needed in public service positions and describe some typical questions.

1) General information

Broad, general information has been found useful for predicting job success in some kinds of work. This is tested in a variety of ways, from vocabulary lists to questions about current events. Basic background in some field of work, such as sociology or economics, may be sampled in a group of questions. Often these are principles which have become familiar to most persons through exposure rather than through formal training. It is difficult to advise you how to study for these questions; being alert to the world around you is our best suggestion.

2) Verbal ability

An example of an ability needed in many positions is verbal or language ability. Verbal ability is, in brief, the ability to use and understand words. Vocabulary and grammar tests are typical measures of this ability. Reading comprehension or paragraph interpretation questions are common in many kinds of civil service tests. You are given a paragraph of written material and asked to find its central meaning.

3) Numerical ability

Number skills can be tested by the familiar arithmetic problem, by checking paired lists of numbers to see which are alike and which are different, or by interpreting charts and graphs. In the latter test, a graph may be printed in the test booklet which you are asked to use as the basis for answering questions.

4) Observation

A popular test for law-enforcement positions is the observation test. A picture is shown to you for several minutes, then taken away. Questions about the picture test your ability to observe both details and larger elements.

5) Following directions

In many positions in the public service, the employee must be able to carry out written instructions dependably and accurately. You may be given a chart with several columns, each column listing a variety of information. The questions require you to carry out directions involving the information given in the chart.

6) Skills and aptitudes

Performance tests effectively measure some manual skills and aptitudes. When the skill is one in which you are trained, such as typing or shorthand, you can practice. These tests are often very much like those given in business school or high school courses. For many of the other skills and aptitudes, however, no short-time preparation can be made. Skills and abilities natural to you or that you have developed throughout your lifetime are being tested.

Many of the general questions just described provide all the data needed to answer the questions and ask you to use your reasoning ability to find the answers. Your best preparation for these tests, as well as for tests of facts and ideas, is to be at your physical and mental best. You, no doubt, have your own methods of getting into an exam-taking mood and keeping "in shape." The next section lists some ideas on this subject.

IV. KINDS OF QUESTIONS

Only rarely is the "essay" question, which you answer in narrative form, used in civil service tests. Civil service tests are usually of the short-answer type. Full instructions for answering these questions will be given to you at the examination. But in case this is your first experience with short-answer questions and separate answer sheets, here is what you need to know:

1) Multiple-choice Questions

Most popular of the short-answer questions is the "multiple choice" or "best answer" question. It can be used, for example, to test for factual knowledge, ability to solve problems or judgment in meeting situations found at work.

A multiple-choice question is normally one of three types—
- It can begin with an incomplete statement followed by several possible endings. You are to find the one ending which *best* completes the statement, although some of the others may not be entirely wrong.
- It can also be a complete statement in the form of a question which is answered by choosing one of the statements listed.

- It can be in the form of a problem – again you select the best answer.

Here is an example of a multiple-choice question with a discussion which should give you some clues as to the method for choosing the right answer:

When an employee has a complaint about his assignment, the action which will *best* help him overcome his difficulty is to
   A. discuss his difficulty with his coworkers
   B. take the problem to the head of the organization
   C. take the problem to the person who gave him the assignment
   D. say nothing to anyone about his complaint

In answering this question, you should study each of the choices to find which is best. Consider choice "A" – Certainly an employee may discuss his complaint with fellow employees, but no change or improvement can result, and the complaint remains unresolved. Choice "B" is a poor choice since the head of the organization probably does not know what assignment you have been given, and taking your problem to him is known as "going over the head" of the supervisor. The supervisor, or person who made the assignment, is the person who can clarify it or correct any injustice. Choice "C" is, therefore, correct. To say nothing, as in choice "D," is unwise. Supervisors have and interest in knowing the problems employees are facing, and the employee is seeking a solution to his problem.

2) True/False Questions

The "true/false" or "right/wrong" form of question is sometimes used. Here a complete statement is given. Your job is to decide whether the statement is right or wrong.

SAMPLE: A roaming cell-phone call to a nearby city costs less than a non-roaming call to a distant city.

This statement is wrong, or false, since roaming calls are more expensive.

This is not a complete list of all possible question forms, although most of the others are variations of these common types. You will always get complete directions for answering questions. Be sure you understand *how* to mark your answers – ask questions until you do.

V. RECORDING YOUR ANSWERS

Computer terminals are used more and more today for many different kinds of exams.
For an examination with very few applicants, you may be told to record your answers in the test booklet itself. Separate answer sheets are much more common. If this separate answer sheet is to be scored by machine – and this is often the case – it is highly important that you mark your answers correctly in order to get credit.
An electronic scoring machine is often used in civil service offices because of the speed with which papers can be scored. Machine-scored answer sheets must be marked with a pencil, which will be given to you. This pencil has a high graphite content which responds to the electronic scoring machine. As a matter of fact, stray dots may register as answers, so do not let your pencil rest on the answer sheet while you are pondering the correct answer. Also, if your pencil lead breaks or is otherwise defective, ask for another.

Since the answer sheet will be dropped in a slot in the scoring machine, be careful not to bend the corners or get the paper crumpled.

The answer sheet normally has five vertical columns of numbers, with 30 numbers to a column. These numbers correspond to the question numbers in your test booklet. After each number, going across the page are four or five pairs of dotted lines. These short dotted lines have small letters or numbers above them. The first two pairs may also have a "T" or "F" above the letters. This indicates that the first two pairs only are to be used if the questions are of the true-false type. If the questions are multiple choice, disregard the "T" and "F" and pay attention only to the small letters or numbers.

Answer your questions in the manner of the sample that follows:

32. The largest city in the United States is
    A. Washington, D.C.
    B. New York City
    C. Chicago
    D. Detroit
    E. San Francisco

1) Choose the answer you think is best. (New York City is the largest, so "B" is correct.)
2) Find the row of dotted lines numbered the same as the question you are answering. (Find row number 32)
3) Find the pair of dotted lines corresponding to the answer. (Find the pair of lines under the mark "B.")
4) Make a solid black mark between the dotted lines.

VI. BEFORE THE TEST

Common sense will help you find procedures to follow to get ready for an examination. Too many of us, however, overlook these sensible measures. Indeed, nervousness and fatigue have been found to be the most serious reasons why applicants fail to do their best on civil service tests. Here is a list of reminders:

- Begin your preparation early – Don't wait until the last minute to go scurrying around for books and materials or to find out what the position is all about.
- Prepare continuously – An hour a night for a week is better than an all-night cram session. This has been definitely established. What is more, a night a week for a month will return better dividends than crowding your study into a shorter period of time.
- Locate the place of the exam – You have been sent a notice telling you when and where to report for the examination. If the location is in a different town or otherwise unfamiliar to you, it would be well to inquire the best route and learn something about the building.
- Relax the night before the test – Allow your mind to rest. Do not study at all that night. Plan some mild recreation or diversion; then go to bed early and get a good night's sleep.
- Get up early enough to make a leisurely trip to the place for the test – This way unforeseen events, traffic snarls, unfamiliar buildings, etc. will not upset you.
- Dress comfortably – A written test is not a fashion show. You will be known by number and not by name, so wear something comfortable.

- Leave excess paraphernalia at home – Shopping bags and odd bundles will get in your way. You need bring only the items mentioned in the official notice you received; usually everything you need is provided. Do not bring reference books to the exam. They will only confuse those last minutes and be taken away from you when in the test room.
- Arrive somewhat ahead of time – If because of transportation schedules you must get there very early, bring a newspaper or magazine to take your mind off yourself while waiting.
- Locate the examination room – When you have found the proper room, you will be directed to the seat or part of the room where you will sit. Sometimes you are given a sheet of instructions to read while you are waiting. Do not fill out any forms until you are told to do so; just read them and be prepared.
- Relax and prepare to listen to the instructions
- If you have any physical problem that may keep you from doing your best, be sure to tell the test administrator. If you are sick or in poor health, you really cannot do your best on the exam. You can come back and take the test some other time.

VII. AT THE TEST

The day of the test is here and you have the test booklet in your hand. The temptation to get going is very strong. Caution! There is more to success than knowing the right answers. You must know how to identify your papers and understand variations in the type of short-answer question used in this particular examination. Follow these suggestions for maximum results from your efforts:

1) Cooperate with the monitor

The test administrator has a duty to create a situation in which you can be as much at ease as possible. He will give instructions, tell you when to begin, check to see that you are marking your answer sheet correctly, and so on. He is not there to guard you, although he will see that your competitors do not take unfair advantage. He wants to help you do your best.

2) Listen to all instructions

Don't jump the gun! Wait until you understand all directions. In most civil service tests you get more time than you need to answer the questions. So don't be in a hurry. Read each word of instructions until you clearly understand the meaning. Study the examples, listen to all announcements and follow directions. Ask questions if you do not understand what to do.

3) Identify your papers

Civil service exams are usually identified by number only. You will be assigned a number; you must not put your name on your test papers. Be sure to copy your number correctly. Since more than one exam may be given, copy your exact examination title.

4) Plan your time

Unless you are told that a test is a "speed" or "rate of work" test, speed itself is usually not important. Time enough to answer all the questions will be provided, but this does not mean that you have all day. An overall time limit has been set. Divide the total time (in minutes) by the number of questions to determine the approximate time you have for each question.

5) Do not linger over difficult questions

If you come across a difficult question, mark it with a paper clip (useful to have along) and come back to it when you have been through the booklet. One caution if you do this – be sure to skip a number on your answer sheet as well. Check often to be sure that you have not lost your place and that you are marking in the row numbered the same as the question you are answering.

6) Read the questions

Be sure you know what the question asks! Many capable people are unsuccessful because they failed to *read* the questions correctly.

7) Answer all questions

Unless you have been instructed that a penalty will be deducted for incorrect answers, it is better to guess than to omit a question.

8) Speed tests

It is often better NOT to guess on speed tests. It has been found that on timed tests people are tempted to spend the last few seconds before time is called in marking answers at random – without even reading them – in the hope of picking up a few extra points. To discourage this practice, the instructions may warn you that your score will be "corrected" for guessing. That is, a penalty will be applied. The incorrect answers will be deducted from the correct ones, or some other penalty formula will be used.

9) Review your answers

If you finish before time is called, go back to the questions you guessed or omitted to give them further thought. Review other answers if you have time.

10) Return your test materials

If you are ready to leave before others have finished or time is called, take ALL your materials to the monitor and leave quietly. Never take any test material with you. The monitor can discover whose papers are not complete, and taking a test booklet may be grounds for disqualification.

VIII. EXAMINATION TECHNIQUES

1) Read the general instructions carefully. These are usually printed on the first page of the exam booklet. As a rule, these instructions refer to the timing of the examination; the fact that you should not start work until the signal and must stop work at a signal, etc. If there are any *special* instructions, such as a choice of questions to be answered, make sure that you note this instruction carefully.

2) When you are ready to start work on the examination, that is as soon as the signal has been given, read the instructions to each question booklet, underline any key words or phrases, such as *least, best, outline, describe* and the like. In this way you will tend to answer as requested rather than discover on reviewing your paper that you *listed without describing*, that you selected the *worst* choice rather than the *best* choice, etc.

3) If the examination is of the objective or multiple-choice type – that is, each question will also give a series of possible answers: A, B, C or D, and you are called upon to select the best answer and write the letter next to that answer on your answer paper – it is advisable to start answering each question in turn. There may be anywhere from 50 to 100 such questions in the three or four hours allotted and you can see how much time would be taken if you read through all the questions before beginning to answer any. Furthermore, if you come across a question or group of questions which you know would be difficult to answer, it would undoubtedly affect your handling of all the other questions.

4) If the examination is of the essay type and contains but a few questions, it is a moot point as to whether you should read all the questions before starting to answer any one. Of course, if you are given a choice – say five out of seven and the like – then it is essential to read all the questions so you can eliminate the two that are most difficult. If, however, you are asked to answer all the questions, there may be danger in trying to answer the easiest one first because you may find that you will spend too much time on it. The best technique is to answer the first question, then proceed to the second, etc.

5) Time your answers. Before the exam begins, write down the time it started, then add the time allowed for the examination and write down the time it must be completed, then divide the time available somewhat as follows:
   - If 3-1/2 hours are allowed, that would be 210 minutes. If you have 80 objective-type questions, that would be an average of 2-1/2 minutes per question. Allow yourself no more than 2 minutes per question, or a total of 160 minutes, which will permit about 50 minutes to review.
   - If for the time allotment of 210 minutes there are 7 essay questions to answer, that would average about 30 minutes a question. Give yourself only 25 minutes per question so that you have about 35 minutes to review.

6) The most important instruction is to *read each question* and make sure you know what is wanted. The second most important instruction is to *time yourself properly* so that you answer every question. The third most important instruction is to *answer every question*. Guess if you have to but include something for each question. Remember that you will receive no credit for a blank and will probably receive some credit if you write something in answer to an essay question. If you guess a letter – say "B" for a multiple-choice question – you may have guessed right. If you leave a blank as an answer to a multiple-choice question, the examiners may respect your feelings but it will not add a point to your score. Some exams may penalize you for wrong answers, so in such cases *only*, you may not want to guess unless you have some basis for your answer.

7) Suggestions
   a. Objective-type questions
      1. Examine the question booklet for proper sequence of pages and questions
      2. Read all instructions carefully
      3. Skip any question which seems too difficult; return to it after all other questions have been answered
      4. Apportion your time properly; do not spend too much time on any single question or group of questions

5. Note and underline key words – *all, most, fewest, least, best, worst, same, opposite,* etc.
6. Pay particular attention to negatives
7. Note unusual option, e.g., unduly long, short, complex, different or similar in content to the body of the question
8. Observe the use of "hedging" words – *probably, may, most likely,* etc.
9. Make sure that your answer is put next to the same number as the question
10. Do not second-guess unless you have good reason to believe the second answer is definitely more correct
11. Cross out original answer if you decide another answer is more accurate; do not erase until you are ready to hand your paper in
12. Answer all questions; guess unless instructed otherwise
13. Leave time for review

  b. Essay questions
    1. Read each question carefully
    2. Determine exactly what is wanted. Underline key words or phrases.
    3. Decide on outline or paragraph answer
    4. Include many different points and elements unless asked to develop any one or two points or elements
    5. Show impartiality by giving pros and cons unless directed to select one side only
    6. Make and write down any assumptions you find necessary to answer the questions
    7. Watch your English, grammar, punctuation and choice of words
    8. Time your answers; don't crowd material

8) Answering the essay question

Most essay questions can be answered by framing the specific response around several key words or ideas. Here are a few such key words or ideas:

M's: manpower, materials, methods, money, management
P's: purpose, program, policy, plan, procedure, practice, problems, pitfalls, personnel, public relations

  a. Six basic steps in handling problems:
    1. Preliminary plan and background development
    2. Collect information, data and facts
    3. Analyze and interpret information, data and facts
    4. Analyze and develop solutions as well as make recommendations
    5. Prepare report and sell recommendations
    6. Install recommendations and follow up effectiveness

  b. Pitfalls to avoid
    1. *Taking things for granted* – A statement of the situation does not necessarily imply that each of the elements is necessarily true; for example, a complaint may be invalid and biased so that all that can be taken for granted is that a complaint has been registered

2. *Considering only one side of a situation* – Wherever possible, indicate several alternatives and then point out the reasons you selected the best one
3. *Failing to indicate follow up* – Whenever your answer indicates action on your part, make certain that you will take proper follow-up action to see how successful your recommendations, procedures or actions turn out to be
4. *Taking too long in answering any single question* – Remember to time your answers properly

IX. AFTER THE TEST

Scoring procedures differ in detail among civil service jurisdictions although the general principles are the same. Whether the papers are hand-scored or graded by machine we have described, they are nearly always graded by number. That is, the person who marks the paper knows only the number – never the name – of the applicant. Not until all the papers have been graded will they be matched with names. If other tests, such as training and experience or oral interview ratings have been given, scores will be combined. Different parts of the examination usually have different weights. For example, the written test might count 60 percent of the final grade, and a rating of training and experience 40 percent. In many jurisdictions, veterans will have a certain number of points added to their grades.

After the final grade has been determined, the names are placed in grade order and an eligible list is established. There are various methods for resolving ties between those who get the same final grade – probably the most common is to place first the name of the person whose application was received first. Job offers are made from the eligible list in the order the names appear on it. You will be notified of your grade and your rank as soon as all these computations have been made. This will be done as rapidly as possible.

People who are found to meet the requirements in the announcement are called "eligibles." Their names are put on a list of eligible candidates. An eligible's chances of getting a job depend on how high he stands on this list and how fast agencies are filling jobs from the list.

When a job is to be filled from a list of eligibles, the agency asks for the names of people on the list of eligibles for that job. When the civil service commission receives this request, it sends to the agency the names of the three people highest on this list. Or, if the job to be filled has specialized requirements, the office sends the agency the names of the top three persons who meet these requirements from the general list.

The appointing officer makes a choice from among the three people whose names were sent to him. If the selected person accepts the appointment, the names of the others are put back on the list to be considered for future openings.

That is the rule in hiring from all kinds of eligible lists, whether they are for typist, carpenter, chemist, or something else. For every vacancy, the appointing officer has his choice of any one of the top three eligibles on the list. This explains why the person whose name is on top of the list sometimes does not get an appointment when some of the persons lower on the list do. If the appointing officer chooses the second or third eligible, the No. 1 eligible does not get a job at once, but stays on the list until he is appointed or the list is terminated.

X. HOW TO PASS THE INTERVIEW TEST

The examination for which you applied requires an oral interview test. You have already taken the written test and you are now being called for the interview test – the final part of the formal examination.

You may think that it is not possible to prepare for an interview test and that there are no procedures to follow during an interview. Our purpose is to point out some things you can do in advance that will help you and some good rules to follow and pitfalls to avoid while you are being interviewed.

What is an interview supposed to test?

The written examination is designed to test the technical knowledge and competence of the candidate; the oral is designed to evaluate intangible qualities, not readily measured otherwise, and to establish a list showing the relative fitness of each candidate – as measured against his competitors – for the position sought. Scoring is not on the basis of "right" and "wrong," but on a sliding scale of values ranging from "not passable" to "outstanding." As a matter of fact, it is possible to achieve a relatively low score without a single "incorrect" answer because of evident weakness in the qualities being measured.

Occasionally, an examination may consist entirely of an oral test – either an individual or a group oral. In such cases, information is sought concerning the technical knowledges and abilities of the candidate, since there has been no written examination for this purpose. More commonly, however, an oral test is used to supplement a written examination.

Who conducts interviews?

The composition of oral boards varies among different jurisdictions. In nearly all, a representative of the personnel department serves as chairman. One of the members of the board may be a representative of the department in which the candidate would work. In some cases, "outside experts" are used, and, frequently, a businessman or some other representative of the general public is asked to serve. Labor and management or other special groups may be represented. The aim is to secure the services of experts in the appropriate field.

However the board is composed, it is a good idea (and not at all improper or unethical) to ascertain in advance of the interview who the members are and what groups they represent. When you are introduced to them, you will have some idea of their backgrounds and interests, and at least you will not stutter and stammer over their names.

What should be done before the interview?

While knowledge about the board members is useful and takes some of the surprise element out of the interview, there is other preparation which is more substantive. It *is* possible to prepare for an oral interview – in several ways:

1) Keep a copy of your application and review it carefully before the interview

This may be the only document before the oral board, and the starting point of the interview. Know what education and experience you have listed there, and the sequence and dates of all of it. Sometimes the board will ask you to review the highlights of your experience for them; you should not have to hem and haw doing it.

2) Study the class specification and the examination announcement

Usually, the oral board has one or both of these to guide them. The qualities, characteristics or knowledges required by the position sought are stated in these documents. They offer valuable clues as to the nature of the oral interview. For example, if the job involves supervisory responsibilities, the announcement will usually indicate that knowledge of modern supervisory methods and the qualifications of the candidate as a supervisor will be tested. If so, you can expect such questions, frequently in the form of a hypothetical situation which you are expected to solve. NEVER go into an oral without knowledge of the duties and responsibilities of the job you seek.

3) Think through each qualification required

Try to visualize the kind of questions you would ask if you were a board member. How well could you answer them? Try especially to appraise your own knowledge and background in each area, *measured against the job sought*, and identify any areas in which you are weak. Be critical and realistic – do not flatter yourself.

4) Do some general reading in areas in which you feel you may be weak

For example, if the job involves supervision and your past experience has NOT, some general reading in supervisory methods and practices, particularly in the field of human relations, might be useful. Do NOT study agency procedures or detailed manuals. The oral board will be testing your understanding and capacity, not your memory.

5) Get a good night's sleep and watch your general health and mental attitude

You will want a clear head at the interview. Take care of a cold or any other minor ailment, and of course, no hangovers.

What should be done on the day of the interview?

Now comes the day of the interview itself. Give yourself plenty of time to get there. Plan to arrive somewhat ahead of the scheduled time, particularly if your appointment is in the fore part of the day. If a previous candidate fails to appear, the board might be ready for you a bit early. By early afternoon an oral board is almost invariably behind schedule if there are many candidates, and you may have to wait. Take along a book or magazine to read, or your application to review, but leave any extraneous material in the waiting room when you go in for your interview. In any event, relax and compose yourself.

The matter of dress is important. The board is forming impressions about you – from your experience, your manners, your attitude, and your appearance. Give your personal appearance careful attention. Dress your best, but not your flashiest. Choose conservative, appropriate clothing, and be sure it is immaculate. This is a business interview, and your appearance should indicate that you regard it as such. Besides, being well groomed and properly dressed will help boost your confidence.

Sooner or later, someone will call your name and escort you into the interview room. *This is it.* From here on you are on your own. It is too late for any more preparation. But remember, you asked for this opportunity to prove your fitness, and you are here because your request was granted.

What happens when you go in?

The usual sequence of events will be as follows: The clerk (who is often the board stenographer) will introduce you to the chairman of the oral board, who will introduce you to the other members of the board. Acknowledge the introductions before you sit down. Do not be surprised if you find a microphone facing you or a stenotypist sitting by. Oral interviews are usually recorded in the event of an appeal or other review.

Usually the chairman of the board will open the interview by reviewing the highlights of your education and work experience from your application – primarily for the benefit of the other members of the board, as well as to get the material into the record. Do not interrupt or comment unless there is an error or significant misinterpretation; if that is the case, do not hesitate. But do not quibble about insignificant matters. Also, he will usually ask you some question about your education, experience or your present job – partly to get you to start talking and to establish the interviewing "rapport." He may start the actual questioning, or turn it over to one of the other members. Frequently, each member undertakes the questioning on a particular area, one in which he is perhaps most competent, so you can expect each member to participate in the examination. Because time is limited, you may also expect some rather abrupt switches in the direction the questioning takes, so do not be upset by it. Normally, a board member will not pursue a single line of questioning unless he discovers a particular strength or weakness.

After each member has participated, the chairman will usually ask whether any member has any further questions, then will ask you if you have anything you wish to add. Unless you are expecting this question, it may floor you. Worse, it may start you off on an extended, extemporaneous speech. The board is not usually seeking more information. The question is principally to offer you a last opportunity to present further qualifications or to indicate that you have nothing to add. So, if you feel that a significant qualification or characteristic has been overlooked, it is proper to point it out in a sentence or so. Do not compliment the board on the thoroughness of their examination – they have been sketchy, and you know it. If you wish, merely say, "No thank you, I have nothing further to add." This is a point where you can "talk yourself out" of a good impression or fail to present an important bit of information. Remember, *you close the interview yourself.*

The chairman will then say, "That is all, Mr. _____, thank you." Do not be startled; the interview is over, and quicker than you think. Thank him, gather your belongings and take your leave. Save your sigh of relief for the other side of the door.

How to put your best foot forward

Throughout this entire process, you may feel that the board individually and collectively is trying to pierce your defenses, seek out your hidden weaknesses and embarrass and confuse you. Actually, this is not true. They are obliged to make an appraisal of your qualifications for the job you are seeking, and they want to see you in your best light. Remember, they must interview all candidates and a non-cooperative candidate may become a failure in spite of their best efforts to bring out his qualifications. Here are 15 suggestions that will help you:

1) Be natural – Keep your attitude confident, not cocky

If you are not confident that you can do the job, do not expect the board to be. Do not apologize for your weaknesses, try to bring out your strong points. The board is interested in a positive, not negative, presentation. Cockiness will antagonize any board member and make him wonder if you are covering up a weakness by a false show of strength.

2) Get comfortable, but don't lounge or sprawl

Sit erectly but not stiffly. A careless posture may lead the board to conclude that you are careless in other things, or at least that you are not impressed by the importance of the occasion. Either conclusion is natural, even if incorrect. Do not fuss with your clothing, a pencil or an ashtray. Your hands may occasionally be useful to emphasize a point; do not let them become a point of distraction.

3) Do not wisecrack or make small talk

This is a serious situation, and your attitude should show that you consider it as such. Further, the time of the board is limited – they do not want to waste it, and neither should you.

4) Do not exaggerate your experience or abilities
   In the first place, from information in the application or other interviews and sources, the board may know more about you than you think. Secondly, you probably will not get away with it. An experienced board is rather adept at spotting such a situation, so do not take the chance.

5) If you know a board member, do not make a point of it, yet do not hide it
   Certainly you are not fooling him, and probably not the other members of the board. Do not try to take advantage of your acquaintanceship – it will probably do you little good.

6) Do not dominate the interview
   Let the board do that. They will give you the clues – do not assume that you have to do all the talking. Realize that the board has a number of questions to ask you, and do not try to take up all the interview time by showing off your extensive knowledge of the answer to the first one.

7) Be attentive
   You only have 20 minutes or so, and you should keep your attention at its sharpest throughout. When a member is addressing a problem or question to you, give him your undivided attention. Address your reply principally to him, but do not exclude the other board members.

8) Do not interrupt
   A board member may be stating a problem for you to analyze. He will ask you a question when the time comes. Let him state the problem, and wait for the question.

9) Make sure you understand the question
   Do not try to answer until you are sure what the question is. If it is not clear, restate it in your own words or ask the board member to clarify it for you. However, do not haggle about minor elements.

10) Reply promptly but not hastily
   A common entry on oral board rating sheets is "candidate responded readily," or "candidate hesitated in replies." Respond as promptly and quickly as you can, but do not jump to a hasty, ill-considered answer.

11) Do not be peremptory in your answers
   A brief answer is proper – but do not fire your answer back. That is a losing game from your point of view. The board member can probably ask questions much faster than you can answer them.

12) Do not try to create the answer you think the board member wants
   He is interested in what kind of mind you have and how it works – not in playing games. Furthermore, he can usually spot this practice and will actually grade you down on it.

13) Do not switch sides in your reply merely to agree with a board member
   Frequently, a member will take a contrary position merely to draw you out and to see if you are willing and able to defend your point of view. Do not start a debate, yet do not surrender a good position. If a position is worth taking, it is worth defending.

14) Do not be afraid to admit an error in judgment if you are shown to be wrong

The board knows that you are forced to reply without any opportunity for careful consideration. Your answer may be demonstrably wrong. If so, admit it and get on with the interview.

15) Do not dwell at length on your present job

The opening question may relate to your present assignment. Answer the question but do not go into an extended discussion. You are being examined for a *new* job, not your present one. As a matter of fact, try to phrase ALL your answers in terms of the job for which you are being examined.

Basis of Rating

Probably you will forget most of these "do's" and "don'ts" when you walk into the oral interview room. Even remembering them all will not ensure you a passing grade. Perhaps you did not have the qualifications in the first place. But remembering them will help you to put your best foot forward, without treading on the toes of the board members.

Rumor and popular opinion to the contrary notwithstanding, an oral board wants you to make the best appearance possible. They know you are under pressure – but they also want to see how you respond to it as a guide to what your reaction would be under the pressures of the job you seek. They will be influenced by the degree of poise you display, the personal traits you show and the manner in which you respond.

ABOUT THIS BOOK

This book contains tests divided into Examination Sections. Go through each test, answering every question in the margin. We have also attached a sample answer sheet at the back of the book that can be removed and used. At the end of each test look at the answer key and check your answers. On the ones you got wrong, look at the right answer choice and learn. Do not fill in the answers first. Do not memorize the questions and answers, but understand the answer and principles involved. On your test, the questions will likely be different from the samples. Questions are changed and new ones added. If you understand these past questions you should have success with any changes that arise. Tests may consist of several types of questions. We have additional books on each subject should more study be advisable or necessary for you. Finally, the more you study, the better prepared you will be. This book is intended to be the last thing you study before you walk into the examination room. Prior study of relevant texts is also recommended. NLC publishes some of these in our Fundamental Series. Knowledge and good sense are important factors in passing your exam. Good luck also helps. So now study this Passbook, absorb the material contained within and take that knowledge into the examination. Then do your best to pass that exam.

EXAMINATION SECTION

EXAMINATION SECTION
TEST 1

DIRECTIONS: Each question or incomplete statement is followed by several suggested answers or completions. Select the one that BEST answers the question or completes the statement. *PRINT THE LETTER OF THE CORRECT ANSWER IN THE SPACE AT THE RIGHT.*

Questions 1-5.

DIRECTIONS: Questions 1 through 5 consist of a sentence with an underlined word. For each question, select the choice that is CLOSEST in meaning to the underlined word.

EXAMPLE
This division reviews the fiscal reports of the agency.
In this sentence, the word *fiscal* means MOST NEARLY
   A. financial   B. critical   C. basic   D. personnel
The correct answer is A. "financial" because "financial" is closest to *fiscal*.
Therefore, the answer is A.

1. Every good office worker needs basic skills.
   The word *basic* in this sentence means
      A. fundamental   B. advanced   C. unusual   D. outstanding

2. He turned out to be a good instructor.
   The word *instructor* in this sentence means
      A. student   B. worker   C. typist   D. teacher

3. The quantity of work in the office was under study.
   In this sentence, the word *quantity* means
      A. amount   B. flow   C. supervision   D. type

4. The morning was spent examining the time records.
   In this sentence, the word *examining* means
      A. distributing   B. collecting   C. checking   D. filing

5. The candidate filled in the proper spaces on the form.
   In this sentence, the word *proper* means
      A. blank   B. appropriate   C. many   D. remaining

1._____

2._____

3._____

4._____

5._____

Questions 6-8.

DIRECTIONS: Questions 6 through 8 are to be answered SOLELY on the basis of the information contained in the following paragraph.

The increase in the number of public documents in the last two centuries closely matches the increase in population in the United States. The great number of public documents has become a serious threat to their usefulness. It is necessary to have programs which will reduce the number of public documents that are kept and which will, at the same time, assure keeping those that have value. Such programs need a great deal of thought to have any success.

6. According to the above paragraph, public documents may be less useful if
   A. the files are open to the public
   B. the record room is too small
   C. the copying machine is operated only during normal working hours
   D. too many records are being kept

7. According to the above paragraph, the growth of the population in the United States has matched the growth in the quantity of public documents for a period of MOST NEARLY _____ years.
   A. 50
   B. 100
   C. 200
   D. 300

8. According to the above paragraph, the increased number of public documents has made it necessary to
   A. find out which public documents are worth keeping
   B. reduce the great number of public documents by decreasing government services
   C. eliminate the copying of all original public documents
   D. avoid all new copying devices

Questions 9-10.

DIRECTIONS: Questions 9 and 10 are to be answered SOLELY on the basis of the information contained in the following paragraph.

The work goals of an agency can best be reached if the employees understand and agree with these goals. One way to gain such understanding and agreement is for management to encourage and seriously consider suggestions from employees in the setting of agency goals.

9. On the basis of the above paragraph, the BEST way to achieve the work goals of an agency is to
   A. make certain that employees work as hard as possible
   B. study the organizational structure of the agency
   C. encourage employees to think seriously about the agency's problems
   D. stimulate employee understanding of the work goals

10. On the basis of the above paragraph, understanding and agreement with agency 10._____
    goals can be gained by
    A. allowing the employees to set agency goals
    B. reaching agency goals quickly
    C. legislative review of agency operations
    D. employee participation in setting agency goals

Questions 11-15.

DIRECTIONS: Each of Questions 11 through 15 consists of a group of four words. One word in each group is incorrectly spelled. For each question, print the letter of the correct answer in the space at the right that is the same as the letter next to the word which is INCORRECTLY spelled.

EXAMPLE

A. housing B. certain C. budgit D. money

The word "budgit" is incorrectly spelled, because the correct spelling should be "budget." Therefore, the correct answer is C.

11.	A. sentince	B. bulletin	C. notice	D. definition	11._____
12.	A. appointment	B. exactly	C. typest	D. light	12._____
13.	A. penalty	B. suparvise	C. consider	D. division	13._____
14.	A. schedule	B. accurate	C. corect	D. simple	14._____
15.	A. suggestion	B. installed	C. proper	D. agincy	15._____

Questions 16-20.

DIRECTIONS: Each Question 16 through 20 consists of a sentence which may be
A. incorrect because of bad word usage, or
B. incorrect because of bad punctuation, or
C. incorrect because of bad spelling, or
D. correct

Read each sentence carefully. Then print in the space at the right A, B, C, or D, according to the answer you choose from the four choices listed above. There is only one type of error in each incorrect sentence. If there is no error, the sentence is correct.

EXAMPLE

George Washington was the father of his contry.
This sentence is incorrect because of bad spelling ("contry" instead of "country"). Therefore, the answer is C.

16. The assignment was completed in record time but the payroll for it has not yet been preparid. 16._____

17. The operator, on the other hand, is willing to learn me how to use the mimeograph. 17._____

18. She is the prettiest of the three sisters. 18._____

19. She doesn't know; if the mail has arrived. 19._____

20. The doorknob of the office door is broke. 20._____

21. A clerk can process a form in 15 minutes.
    How many forms can that clerk process in six hours?
    A. 10   B. 21   C. 24   D. 90   21._____

22. An office staff consists of 120 people. Sixty of them have been assigned to a special project. Of the remaining staff, 20 answer the mail, 10 handle phone calls, and the rest operate the office machines.
    The number of people operating the office machines is
    A. 20   B. 30   C. 40   D. 45   22._____

23. An office worker received 65 applications but on the first day had to return 26 of them for being incomplete and on the second day 25 had to be returned for being incomplete.
    How many applications did NOT have to be returned?
    A. 10   B. 12   C. 14   D. 16   23._____

24. An office worker answered 63 phone calls in one day and 91 phone calls the next day.
    For these 2 days, what was the average number of phone calls he answered per day?
    A. 77   B. 28   C. 82   D. 93   24._____

25. An office worker processed 12 vouchers of $8.50 each, 3 vouchers of $3.68 each, and 2 vouchers of $1.29 each.
    The TOTAL dollar amount of these vouchers is
    A. $116.04   B. $117.52   C. $118.62   D. $119.04   25._____

KEY (CORRECT ANSWERS)

1.	A	11.	A
2.	D	12.	C
3.	A	13.	B
4.	C	14.	C
5.	B	15.	D
6.	D	16.	C
7.	C	17.	A
8.	A	18.	D
9.	D	19.	B
10.	D	20.	A

21. C
22. B
23. C
24. A
25. C

TEST 2

DIRECTIONS: Each question or incomplete statement is followed by several suggested answers or completions. Select the one that BEST answers the question or completes the statement. *PRINT THE LETTER OF THE CORRECT ANSWER IN THE SPACE AT THE RIGHT.*

Questions 1-5.

DIRECTIONS: Each Question from 1 through 5 lists four names. The names may not be exactly the same. Compare the names in each question and mark your answer
- A if all the names are different
- B if only two names are exactly the same
- C if only three names are exactly the same
- D if all four names are exactly the same

EXAMPLE
Jensen, Alfred E.
Jensen, Alfred E.
Jensan, Alfred E.
Jensen, Fred E.

Since the name Jensen, Alfred E. appears twice and is exactly the same in both places, the correct answer is B.

1. A. Riviera, Pedro S.   B. Rivers, Pedro S.   1.____
    C. Riviera, Pedro N.   D. Riviera, Juan S.

2. A. Guider, Albert   B. Guidar, Albert   2.____
    C. Giuder, Alfred   D. Guider, Albert

3. A. Blum, Rona   B. Blum, Rona   3.____
    C. Blum, Rona   D. Blum, Rona

4. A. Raugh, John   B. Raugh, James   4.____
    C. Raughe, John   D. Raugh, John

5. A. Katz, Stanley   B. Katz, Stanley   5.____
    C. Katze, Stanley   D. Katz, Stanley

Questions 6-10.

DIRECTIONS: Each Question 6 through 10 consists of numbers or letters in Columns I and II. For each question, compare each line of Column I with its corresponding line in Column II and decide how many lines in Column I are EXACTLY the same as their corresponding lines in Column II. In your answer space, mark your answer
- A if only ONE line in Column I is exactly the same as its corresponding line in Column II
- B if only TWO lines in Column I are exactly the same as their corresponding lines in Column II

C if only THREE lines in Column I are exactly the same as their corresponding lines in Column II
D if all FOUR lines in Column I are exactly the same as their corresponding lines in Column II

EXAMPLE

Column I	Column II
1776	1776
1865	1865
1945	1945
1976	1978

Only three lines in Column I are exactly the same as their corresponding lines in Column II. Therefore, the correct answer is C.

	Column I	Column II	
6.	5653	5653	6._____
	8727	8728	
	ZPSS	ZPSS	
	4952	9453	
7.	PNJP	PNPJ	7._____
	NJPJ	NJPJ	
	JNPN	JNPN	
	PNJP	PNPJ	
8.	effe	eFfe	8._____
	uWvw	uWvw	
	KpGj	KpGg	
	vmnv	vmnv	
9.	5232	5232	9._____
	PfrC	PfrN	
	zssz	zzss	
	rwwr	rwww	
10.	czws	czws	10._____
	cecc	cece	
	thrm	thrm	
	lwtz	lwtz	

Questions 11-15.

DIRECTIONS: Questions 11 through 15 have lines of letters and numbers. Each letter should be matched with its number in accordance with the following table.

Letter	F	R	C	A	W	L	E	N	B	T
Matching Number	0	1	2	3	4	5	6	7	8	9

From the table you can determine that the letter F has the matching number 0 below it, the letter R has the matching number 1 below, etc.

For each question, compare each line of letters and numbers carefully to see if each letter has its correct matching number. If all the letters and numbers are matched correctly in

    none of the lines of the question, mark your answer A
    only *one* of the lines of the question, mark your answer B
    only *two* of the lines of the question, mark your answer C
    all three lines of the question, mark your answer D

EXAMPLE

WBCR	4826
TLBF	9580
ATNE	3986

There is a mistake in the first line because the letter R should have its matching number 1 instead of the number 6.

The second line is correct because each letter shown has the correct matching number.

There is a mistake in the third line because the letter N should have the matching number 7 instead of the number 8.

Since all the letters and numbers are correct matched in only one of the lines in the sample, the correct answer is B.

11. EBCT   6829
    ATWR   3961
    NLBW   7584

11.____

12. RNCT   1729
    LNCR   5728
    WAEB   5368

12.____

13. NTWB   7948
    RABL   1385
    TAEF   9360

13.____

14. LWRB   5417
    RLWN   1647
    CBWA   2843

14.____

15. ABTC   3792
    WCER   5261
    AWCN   3417

15.____

16. Your job often brings you into contact with the public.
Of the following, it would be MOST desirable to explain the reasons for official actions to people coming into your office for assistance because such explanations
    A. help build greater understanding between the public and your agency
    B. help build greater self-confidence in city employees
    C. convince the public that nothing they do can upset a city employee
    D. show the public that city employees are intelligent

16.____

17. Assume that you strongly dislike one of your co-workers.
    You should FIRST
    A. discuss your feeling with the co-worker
    B. demand a transfer to another office
    C. suggest to your supervisor that the co-worker should be observed carefully
    D. try to figure out the reason for this dislike before you say or do anything

18. An office worker who has problems accepting authority is MOST likely to find it difficult to
    A. obey rules
    B. understand people
    C. assist other employees
    D. follow complex instructions

19. The employees in your office have taken a dislike to one person and frequently annoy her.
    Your supervisor should
    A. transfer this person to another unit at the first opportunity
    B. try to find out the reason for the staff's attitude before doing anything about it
    C. threaten to transfer the first person observed bothering this person
    D. ignore the situation

20. Assume that your supervisor has asked a worker in your office to get a copy of a report out of the files. You notice the worker as accidentally pulled out the wrong report.
    Of the following, the BEST way for you to handle this situation is to tell
    A. the worker about all the difficulties that will result from this error
    B. the worker about her mistake in a nice way
    C. the worker to ignore this error
    D. your supervisor that this worker needs more training in how to use the files

21. Filing systems differ in their efficiency.
    Which of the following is the BEST way to evaluate the efficiency of a filing system? A
    A. number of times used per day
    B. amount of material that is received each day for filing
    C. amount of time it takes to locate material
    D. type of locking system used

22. In planning ahead so that a sufficient amount of general office supplies is always available, it would be LEAST important to find out the
    A. current office supply needs of the staff
    B. amount of office supplies used last year
    C. days and times that office supplies can be ordered
    D. agency goals and objectives

23. The MAIN reason for establishing routine office work procedures is that once a routine is established
    A. work need not be checked for accuracy
    B. all steps in the routine will take an equal amount of time to perform
    C. each time the job is repeated, it will take less time to perform
    D. each step in the routine will not have to be planned all over again each time

24. When an office machine centrally located in an agency must be shut down for repairs, the bureaus and divisions using this machine should be informed of the
    A. expected length of time before the machine will be in operation again
    B. estimated cost of repairs
    C. efforts being made to avoid future repairs
    D. type of new equipment which the agency may buy in the future to replace the machine being repaired

25. If the day's work is properly scheduled, the MOST important result would be that the
    A. supervisor will not have to do much supervision
    B. employee will know what to do next
    C. employee will show greater initiative
    D. job will become routine

KEY (CORRECT ANSWERS)

1.	A		11.	C
2.	B		12.	B
3.	D		13.	D
4.	B		14.	B
5.	C		15.	A
6.	B		16.	A
7.	B		17.	D
8.	B		18.	A
9.	A		19.	B
10.	C		20.	B

21. C
22. D
23. D
24. A
25. B

EXAMINATION SECTION
TEST 1

DIRECTIONS: Each question or incomplete statement is followed by several suggested answers or completions. Select the one that BEST answers the question or completes the statement. *PRINT THE LETTER OF THE CORRECT ANSWER IN THE SPACE AT THE RIGHT.*

Questions 1-2.

DIRECTIONS: Questions 1 and 2 are to be answered on the basis of the following conditions.

Assume that you work for Department A, which occupies several floors in one building. There is a reception office on each floor. All visitors (persons not employed in the department) are required to go to the reception office on the same floor as the office of the person they want to see. They sign a register, their presence is announced by the receptionist, and they wait in the reception room for the person they are visiting.

1. As you are walking in the corridor of your department on your way to a meeting in Room 314, a visitor approaches you and asks you to direct her to Room 312. She says that she is delivering some papers to Mr. Crane in that office. The MOST APPROPRIATE action for you to take is to

    A. offer to deliver the papers to Mr. Crane since you will be passing his office
    B. suggest that she come with you since you will be passing Room 312
    C. direct her to the reception office where Mr. Crane will be contacted for her
    D. take her to the reception office and contact Mr. Crane for her

    1.____

2. You are acting as receptionist in the reception office on the second floor. A man enters, stating that he is an accountant from another department and that he has an appointment with Mr. Prince, who is located in Room 102 on the first floor.
   The BEST action for you to take is to

    A. phone the reception office on the first floor and ask the receptionist to contact Mr. Prince
    B. advise the man to go to the reception office on the first floor where he will be further assisted
    C. contact Mr. Prince for him and ask that he come to your office where his visitor is waiting
    D. send him directly to Room 102 where he can see Mr. Prince

    2.____

3. One of the employees whom you supervise complains to you that you give her more work than the other employees and that she cannot finish these assignments by the time you expect them to be completed.
   Of the following, the FIRST action you should then take is to

    A. tell the employee that you expect more work from her because the other employees do not have her capabilities
    B. assure the employee that you always divide the work equally among your subordinates

    3.____

11

C. review the employee's recent assignments in order to determine whether her complaint is justified
D. ask the employee if there are any personal problems which are interfering with the completion of the assignments

4. Assume that a staff regulation exists which requires an employee to inform his supervisor if the employee will be absent on a particular day.
If an employee fails to follow this regulation, the FIRST action his supervisor should take is to

   A. inform his own supervisor of the situation and ask for further instructions
   B. ask the employee to explain his failure to follow the regulation
   C. tell the employee that another breach of the regulation will lead to disciplinary action
   D. reprimand the employee for failing to follow the regulation

5. An employee tells his supervisor that he submitted an idea to the employees' suggestion program by mail over two months ago and still has not received an indication that the suggestion is being considered. The employee states that when one of his co-workers sent in a suggestion, he received a response within one week. The employee then asks his supervisor what he should do.
Which of the following is the BEST response for the supervisor to make?

   A. "Next time you have a suggestion, see me about it first and I will make sure that it is properly handled."
   B. "I'll try to find out whether your suggestion was received by the program and whether a response was sent."
   C. "Your suggestion probably wasn't that good so there's no sense in pursuing the matter any further."
   D. "Let's get together and submit the suggestion jointly so that it will carry more weight."

6. Assume that you have been trying to teach a newly appointed employee the filing procedures used in your office. The employee seems to be having difficulty learning the procedures even though you consider them relatively simple and you originally learned them in less time than you have already spent trying to teach the new employee.
Before you spend any time trying to teach him any new filing procedures, which of the following actions should you take FIRST?

   A. Try to teach him some other aspect of your office's work.
   B. Tell him that you had little difficulty learning the procedures and ask him why he finds them so hard to learn.
   C. Review with him those procedures you have tried to teach him and determine whether he understands them.
   D. Report to your supervisor that the new employee is unsuited for the work performed in your office.

7. There is a rule in your office that all employees must sign in and out for lunch. You notice that a new employee who is under your direct supervision has not signed in or out for lunch for the past three days. Of the following, the MOST effective action to take is to

A. immediately report this matter to your supervisor
B. note this infraction of rules on the employee's personnel record
C. remind the employee that she must sign in and out for lunch every day
D. send around a memorandum to all employees in the office telling them they must sign in and out for lunch every day

Questions 8-15.

DIRECTIONS: Questions 8 through 15 each show in Column I names written on four cards (lettered w, x, y, z) which have to be filed. You are to choose the option (lettered A, B, C, or D) in Column II which BEST represents the proper order of filing according to the rules and sample question given below. The cards are to be filed according to the following Rules for Alphabetical Filing.

RULES FOR ALPHABETICAL FILING

Names of Individuals

1. The names of individuals are filed in strict alphabetical order, first according to the last name, then according to first name or initial, and finally according to middle name or initial. For example: George Allen precedes Edward Bell and Leonard Reston precedes Lucille Reston.

2. When last names are the same, for example, A. Green and Agnes Green, the one with the initial comes before the one with the name written out when the first initials are identical.

3. When first and last names are the same, a name without a middle initial comes before one with a middle initial. For example: Ralph Simon comes before both Ralph A. Simon and Ralph Adam Simon.

4. When first and last names are the same, a name with a middle initial comes before one with a middle name beginning with the same initial. For example: Sam P. Rogers comes before Sam Paul Rogers.

5. Prefixes such as De, 0', Mac, Mc, and Van are filed as written and are treated as part of the names to which they are connected. For example: Gladys McTeaque is filed before Frances Meadows.

6. Abbreviated names are treated as if they were spelled out. For example: Chas. is filed as Charles and Thos. is filed as Thomas.

7. Titles and designations such as Dr., Mr., and Prof, are ignored in filing.

Names of Organizations

1. The names of business organizations are filed according to the order in which each word in the name appears. When an organization name bears the name of a person, it is filed according to the rules for filing names of people as given above. Vivian Quinn Boutique would, therefore, come before Security Locks Inc. because Quinn comes before Security.

2. When numerals occur in a name, they are treated as if they were spelled out. For example: 4th Street Thrift Shop is filed as Fourth Street Thrift Shop.

3. When the following words are part of the name of an organization, they are ignored: on, the, of, and.

SAMPLE

	Column I	Column II	The correct way to file the cards is:
w.	Jane Earl	A. w, y, z, x	y. James Earl
x.	James A. Earle	B. y, w, z, x	w. Jane Earl
y.	James Earl	C. x, y, w, z	z. J. Earle
z.	J. Earle	D. x, w, y, z	x. James A. Earle

The correct filing order is shown by the letters, y, w, z, x (in that sequence). Since, in Column II, B appears in front of the letters, y, w, z, x (in that sequence), B is the correct answer to the sample question.

Now answer the following questions using that same procedure.

		Column I		Column II
8.	w.	James Rothschild	A.	x, z, w, y
	x.	Julius B. Rothchild	B.	x, w, z, y
	y.	B. Rothstein	C.	z, y, w, x
	z.	Brian Joel Rothenstein	D.	z, w, x, y
9.	w.	George S. Wise	A.	w, y, z, x
	x.	S. G. Wise	B.	x, w, y, z
	y.	Geo. Stuart Wise	C.	y, x, w, z
	z.	Prof. Diana Wise	D.	z, w, y, x
10.	w.	10th Street Bus Terminal	A.	x, z, w, y
	x.	Buckingham Travel Agency	B.	y, x, w, z
	y.	The Buckingham Theater	C.	w, z, y, x
	z.	Burt Tompkins Studio	D.	x, w, y, z
11.	w.	National Council of American Importers	A.	w, y, x, z
	x.	National Chain Co. of Providence	B.	x, z, w, y
			C.	z, x, w, y
	y.	National Council on Alcoholism	D.	z, x, y, w
	z.	National Chain Co.		
12.	w.	Dr. Herbert Alvary	A.	w, y, x, z
	x.	Mr. Victor Alvarado	B.	z, w, x, y
	y.	Alvar Industries	C.	y, z, x, w
	z.	V. Alvarado	D.	w, z, x, y

	Column I		Column II	
13.	w. Joan MacBride x. Wm. Mackey y. Roslyn McKenzie z. Winifred Mackey		A. w, x, z, y B. w, y, z, x C. w, z, x, y D. w, y, x, z	13._____

	Column I		Column II	
14.	w. 3 Way Trucking Co. x. 3rd Street Bakery y. 380 Realty Corp. z. Three Lions Pub		A. y, x, z, w B. y, z, w, x C. x, y, z, w D. x, y, w, z	14._____
15.	w. Miss Rose Leonard x. Rev. Leonard Lucas y. Sylvia Leonard Linen Shop z. Rose S. Leonard		A. z, w, x, y B. w, z, y, x C. w, x, z, y D. z, w, y, x	15._____

Questions 16-19.

DIRECTIONS: Answer Questions 16 through 19 ONLY on the basis of the information given in the following passage.

Work measurement concerns accomplishment or productivity. It has to do with results; it does not deal with the amount of energy used up, although in many cases this may be in direct proportion to the work output. Work measurement not only helps a manager to distribute work loads fairly, but it also enables him to define work sueeess in actual units, evaluate employee performance, and determine where corrective help is needed. Work measurement is accomplished by measuring the amount produced, measuring the time spent to produce it, and relating the two. To illustrate, it is common to speak of so many orders processed within a given time. The number of orders processed becomes meaningful when related to the amount of time taken.

Much of the work in an office can be measured fairly accurately and inexpensively. The extent of wo.rk measurement possible in any given case will depend upon the particular type of office tasks performed, but usually from two-thirds to three-fourths of all work in an office can be measured. It is true that difficulty in work measurement is encountered, for example, when the office work is irregular and not repeated often, or when the work is primarily mental rather than manual. These are problems, but they are used as excuses for doing no work measurement far more frequently than is justified.

16. According to the above passage, which of the following BEST illustrates the type of information obtained as a result of work measurement? A   16._____

   A. clerk takes one hour to file 150 folders
   B. typist types five letters
   C. stenographer works harder typing from shorthand notes than she does typing from a typed draft
   D. clerk keeps track of employees' time by computing sick leave, annual leave, and overtime leave

17. The above passage does NOT indicate that work measurement can be used to help a supervisor to determine

   A. why an employee is performing poorly on the job
   B. who are the fast and slow workers in the unit
   C. how the work in the unit should be divided up
   D. how long it should take to perform a certain task

17.____

18. According to the above passage, the kind of work that would be MOST difficult to measure would be such work as

   A. sorting mail
   B. designing a form for a new procedure
   C. photocopying various materials
   D. answering inquiries with form letters

18.____

19. The excuses mentioned in the above passage for failure to perform work measurement can be BEST summarized as the

   A. repetitive nature of office work
   B. costs involved in carrying out accurate work measurement
   C. inability to properly use the results obtained from work measurement
   D. difficulty involved in measuring certain types of work

19.____

Questions 20-24.

DIRECTIONS: In each of Questions 20 through 24, there is a sentence containing one underlined word. Choose the word (lettered A, B, C, or D) which means MOST NEARLY the same as the underlined word as it is used in the sentence.

20. Mr. Warren could not attend the luncheon because he had a prior appointment.

   A. conflicting   B. official
   C. previous   D. important

20.____

21. The time allowed to complete the task was not adequate.

   A. long   B. enough   C. excessive   D. required

21.____

22. The investigation unit began an extensive search for the information.

   A. complicated   B. superficial
   C. thorough   D. leisurely

22.____

23. The secretary answered the telephone in a courteous manner.

   A. businesslike   B. friendly
   C. formal   D. polite

23.____

24. The recipient of the money checked the total amount.

   A. receiver   B. carrier   C. borrower   D. giver

24.____

25. You receive a telephone call from an employee in another agency requesting information about a project being carried out by a division other than your own. You know little about the work being done, but you would like to help the caller.
Of the following, the BEST action for you to take is to

   A. ask the caller exactly what he would like to know and then tell him all you know about the work being done
   B. ask the caller to tell you exactly what he would like to know so that you can get the information while he waits
   C. tell the caller that you will have the call transferred to the division working on the project
   D. request that the caller write to you so that you can send him the necessary information

25._____

KEY (CORRECT ANSWERS)

1. C
2. B
3. C
4. B
5. B

6. C
7. C
8. A
9. D
10. B

11. D
12. C
13. A
14. C
15. B

16. A
17. A
18. B
19. D
20. C

21. B
22. C
23. D
24. A
25. C

TEST 2

DIRECTIONS: Each question or incomplete statement is followed by several suggested answers or completions. Select the one that BEST answers the question or completes the statement. *PRINT THE LETTER OF THE CORRECT ANSWER IN THE SPACE AT THE RIGHT.*

1. Which of the following actions by a supervisor is LEAST likely to result in an increase in morale or productivity?   1.____

    A. Delegating additional responsibility but not authority to his subordinates
    B. Spending more time than his subordinates in planning and organizing the office's work
    C. Giving positive rather than negative orders to his subordinates
    D. Keeping his subordinates informed about changes in rules or policies which affect their work

Questions 2-8.

DIRECTIONS: Questions 2 through 8 are based SOLELY on the information and the form given below.

The following form is a Weekly Summary of New Employees and lists all employees appointed to Department F in the week indicated. In addition to the starting date and name, the form includes each new employee's time card number, title, status, work location and supervisor's name.

DEPARTMENT F						
Weekly Summary of New Employees					Week Starting March 25	
Starting Date	Name Last, First	Time Card No.	Title	Status	Work Location	Supervisor
3/25	Astaire, Hannah	361	Typist	Prov.	Rm. 312	Merrill, Judy
3/25	Silber, Arthur	545	Clerk	Perm.	Rm. 532	Rizzo, Joe
3/26	Vecchio, Robert	620	Accountant	Perm.	Rm. 620	Harper, Ruth
3/26	Goldberg, Sally	373	Stenographer	Prov.	Rm. 308	Merrill, Judy
3/26	Yee, Bruce	555	Accountant	Perm.	Rm. 530	Rizzo, Joe
3/27	Dunning, Betty	469	Typist	Perm.	Rm. 411	Miller, Tony
3/28	Goldman, Sara	576	Stenographer	Prov.	Rm. 532	Rizzo, Joe
3/29	Vesquez, Roy	624	Accountant	Perm.	Rm. 622	Harper, Ruth
3/29	Browning, David	464	Typist	Perm.	Rm. 411	Miller, Tony

18

2. On which one of the following dates did two employees *in the same title* begin work? 2.____

   A. 3/25   B. 3/26   C. 3/27   D. 3/29

3. To which one of the following supervisors was ONE typist assigned? 3.____

   A. Judy Merrill B. Tony Miller
   C. Ruth Harper D. Joe Rizzo

4. Which one of the following supervisors was assigned the GREATEST number of new employees during the week of March 25? 4.____

   A. Ruth Harper B. Judy Merrill
   C. Tony Miller D. Joe Rizzo

5. Which one of the following employees was assigned *three days after another employee* to the same job location? 5.____

   A. Sara Goldman B. David Browning
   C. Bruce Yee D. Roy Vesquez

6. The title in which BOTH provisional and permanent appointments were made is 6.____

   A. accountant   B. clerk   C. stenographer   D. typist

7. The employee who started work on the SAME day and have the SAME status but DIFFERENT titles are 7.____

   A. Arthur Silber and Hannah Astaire
   B. Robert Vecchio and Bruce Yee
   C. Sally Goldberg and Sara Goldman
   D. Roy Vesquez and David Browning

8. On the basis of the information given on the form, which one of the following conclusions regarding time card numbers appears to be CORRECT? 8.____

   A. The first digit of the time card number is coded according to the assigned title.
   B. The middle digit of the time card number is coded according to the assigned title.
   C. The first digit of the time card number is coded according to the employees' floor locations.
   D. Time card numbers are randomly assigned.

9. Assume that a caller arrives at your desk and states that she is your supervisor's daughter and that she would like to see her father. You have been under the impression that your supervisor has only a two-year-old son.
   Of the following, the BEST way to deal with this visitor is to 9.____

   A. offer her a seat and advise your supervisor of the visitor
   B. tell her to go right in to her father's office
   C. ask her for some proof to show that she is your supervisor's daughter
   D. escort her into your supervisor's office and ask him if the visitor is his daughter

10. Assume that you answer the telephone and the caller says that he is a police officer and asks for personal information about one of your co-workers.
    Of the following, the BEST course of action for you to take is to 10.____

A. give the caller the information he has requested
B. ask the caller for the telephone number of the phone he is using, call him back, and then give him the information
C. refuse to give him any information and offer to transfer the call to your supervisor
D. ask the caller for his name and badge number before giving him the information

Questions 11-16.

DIRECTIONS: Questions 11 through 16 each consist of a sentence which may or may not be an example of good English usage. Consider grammar, punctuation, spelling, capitalization, awkwardness, etc. Examine each sentence, and then choose the correct statement about it from the four choices below it. If the English usage in the sentence given is better than it would be with any of the changes suggested in Options B, C, or D, choose Option A. Do not choose an option that will change the meaning of the sentence.

11. The recruiting officer said, "There are many different goverment jobs available." 11.____
    A. This is an example of acceptable writing.
    B. The word *There* should not be capitalized.
    C. The word *goverment* should be spelled *government*.
    D. The comma after the word *said* should be removed.

12. He can recommend a mechanic whose work is reliable. 12.____
    A. This is an example of acceptable writing.
    B. The word *reliable* should be spelled *relyable*.
    C. The word *whose* should be spelled *who's*.
    D. The word *mechanic* should be spelled *mecanic*.

13. She typed quickly; like someone who had not a moment to lose. 13.____
    A. This is an example of acceptable writing.
    B. The word *not* should be removed.
    C. The semicolon should be changed to a comma.
    D. The word *quickly* should be placed before instead of after the word *typed*.

14. She insisted that she had to much work to do. 14.____
    A. This is an example of acceptable writing.
    B. The word *insisted* should be spelled *incisted*.
    C. The word *to* used in front of *much* should be spelled *too*.
    D. The word *do* should be changed to *be done*.

15. He excepted praise from his supervisor for a job well done. 15.____
    A. This is an example of acceptable writing.
    B. The word *excepted* should be spelled *accepted*.
    C. The order of the words *well done* should be changed to *done well*.
    D. There should be a comma after the word *supervisor*

16. What appears to be intentional errors in grammar occur several times in the passage.   16._____

    A. This is an example of acceptable writing.
    B. The word *occur* should be spelled *occurr*.
    C. The word *appears* should be changed to *appear*.
    D. The phrase *several times* should be changed to *from time to time*.

17. The daily compensation to be paid to each consultant hired in a certain agency is computed by dividing his professional earnings in the previous year by 250. The maximum daily compensation they can receive is $200 each. Four consultants who were hired to work on a special project had the following professional earnings in the previous year: $37,500, $44,000, $46,500, and $61,100.   17._____
    What will be the TOTAL DAILY COST to the agency for these four consultants?

    A. $932   B. $824   C. $756   D. $712

18. In a typing and stenographic pool consisting of 30 employees, 2/5 of them are typists, 1/3 of them are senior typists and senior stenographers, and the rest are stenographers. If there are 5 more stenographers than senior stenographers, how many senior stenographers are in the typing and stenographic pool?   18._____

    A. 3   B. 5   C. 8   D. 10

19. There are 3330 copies of a three-page report to be collated. One clerk starts collating at 9:00 A.M. and is joined 15 minutes later by two other clerks. It takes 15 minutes for each of these clerks to collate 90 copies of the report.   19._____
    At what time should the job be completed if ALL three clerks continue working at the SAME rate without breaks?

    A. 12:00 Noon   B. 12:15 P.M.   C. 1:00 P.M.   D. 1:15 P.M.

20. By the end of last year, membership in the blood credit program in a certain agency had increased from the year before by 500, bringing the total to 2500.   20._____
    If the membership increased by the same percentage this year, the TOTAL number of members in the blood credit program for this agency by the end of this year should be

    A. 2625   B. 3000   C. 3125   D. 3250

21. During this year, an agency suggestion program put into practice suggestions from 24 employees, thereby saving the agency 40 times the amount of money it paid in awards. If 1/3 of the employees were awarded $50 each, 1/2 of the employees were awarded $25 each, and the rest were awarded $10 each, how much money did the agency SAVE by using the suggestions?   21._____

    A. $18,760   B. $29,600   C. $32,400   D. $46,740

22. Which of the following actions should a supervisor generally find MOST effective as a method of determining whether subordinates need additional training in performing their work?   22._____

    A. Compiling a list of absences and latenesses of subordinates
    B. Observing the manner in which his subordinates carry out their various tasks
    C. Reviewing the grievances submitted by subordinates
    D. Reminding his subordinates to consult him if they experience difficulty in completing an assignment

23. Of the following types of letters, the MOST difficult to trace if lost after mailing is the _____ letter.

    A. special delivery
    B. registered
    C. insured
    D. certified

24. Suppose that you are looking over a few incoming letters that have been put in your mail basket. You see that one has a return address on the envelope but not on the letter itself. Of the following, the BEST way to make sure there is a correct record of the return address is to

    A. return the letter to the sender and ask him to fill in his address on his own letter
    B. put the letter back into the envelope and close the opening with a paper clip
    C. copy the address onto a 3"x5" index card and throw away the envelope
    D. copy the address onto the letter and staple the envelope to the letter

25. Although most incoming mail that you receive in an office will pertain to business matters, there are times when a letter may be delivered for your supervisor that is marked *Personal*.
    Of the following, the BEST way for you to handle this type of mail is to

    A. open the letter but do not read it, and route it along with the other mail
    B. read the letter to see if it really is personal
    C. have the letter forwarded unopened to your supervisor's home address
    D. deliver the letter to your supervisor's desk unopened

KEY (CORRECT ANSWERS)

1.	A	11.	C
2.	B	12.	A
3.	A	13.	C
4.	D	14.	C
5.	A	15.	B
6.	D	16.	C
7.	D	17.	D
8.	C	18.	A
9.	A	19.	B
10.	C	20.	C

21.	B
22.	B
23.	D
24.	D
25.	D

EXAMINATION SECTION
TEST 1

DIRECTIONS: Each question or incomplete statement is followed by several suggested answers or completions. Select the one that BEST answers the question or completes the statement. *PRINT THE LETTER OF THE CORRECT ANSWER IN THE SPACE AT THE RIGHT.*

1. A supervisor may be required to help train a newly appointed clerk. Which of the following is LEAST important for a newly appointed clerk to know in order to perform his work efficiently?
   A. Acceptable ways of answering and recording telephone calls
   B. The number of files in the storage files unit
   C. The filing methods used by his unit
   D. Proper techniques for handling visitors

   1.____

2. In your agency you have the responsibility of processing clients who have appointments with agency representatives. On a particularly busy day, a client comes to your desk and insists that she must see the person handling her case although she has no appointment.
   Under the circumstances, your FIRST action should be to
   A. show her the full appointment schedule
   B. give her an appointment for another day
   C. ask her to explain the urgency
   D. tell her to return later in the day

   2.____

3. Which of the following practices is BEST for a supervisor to use when assigning work to his staff?
   A. Give workers with seniority the most difficult jobs
   B. Assign all unimportant work to the slower workers
   C. Permit each employee to pick the job he prefers
   D. Make assignments based on the workers' abilities

   3.____

4. In which of the following instances is a supervisor MOST justified in giving commands to people under his supervision? When
   A. they delay in following instructions which have been given to them clearly
   B. they become relaxed and slow about work, and he wants to speed up their production
   C. he must direct them in an emergency situation
   D. he is instructing them on jobs that are unfamiliar to them

   4.____

5. Which of the following supervisory actions or attitudes is MOST likely to result in getting subordinates to try to do as much work as possible for a supervisor? He
   A. shows that his most important interest is in schedules and production goals
   B. consistently pressures his staff to get the work out

   5.____

2 (#1)

    C. never fails to let them know he is in charge
    D. considers their abilities and needs while requiring that production goals be met

6. Assume that a supervisor has been explaining certain regulations to a new clerk under his supervision.
The MOST efficient way for the supervisor to make sure that the clerk has understood the explanation is to
    A. give him written materials on the regulations
    B. ask him if he has any further questions about the regulations
    C. ask him specific questions based on what has just been explained to him
    D. watch the way he handles a situation involving these regulations

7. One of your unit clerks has been assigned to work for a Mr. Jones in another office for several days. At the end of the first day, Mr. Jones, saying the clerk was not satisfactory, asks that she not be assigned to him again. This clerk is one of your most dependable workers, and no previous complaints about her work have come to you from any other outside assignments.
To get to the root of this situation, your FIRST action should be to
    A. ask Mr. Jones to explain in what way her work was unsatisfactory
    B. ask the clerk what she did that Mr. Jones considered unsatisfactory
    C. check with supervisors for whom she previously worked to see if your own rating of her is in error
    D. tell Mr. Jones to pick the clerk he would prefer to have work for him the next time

8. A senior typist, still on probation, is instructed to type, as quickly as possible, one section of a draft of a long, complex report. Her part must be typed and readable before another part of the report can be written. Asked when she can have the report ready, she gives her supervisor an estimate of a day longer than she knows it will actually take. She then finishes the job a day sooner than the date given her supervisor.
The judgment shown by the senior typist in giving an overestimate of time in a situation like this is, in general,
    A. *good*, because it prevents the supervisor from thinking she works slowly
    B. *good*, because it keeps unrealistic supervisors from expecting too much
    C. *bad*, because she should have used the time left to further check and proofread her work
    D. *bad*, because schedules and plans for other parts of the project may have been based on her false estimate

9. Suppose a new clerk, still on probation, is placed under your supervision and refuses to do a job you ask him to do.
What is the FIRST thing you should do?
    A. Explain that you are the supervisor and he must follow your instructions
    B. Tell him he may be suspended if he refuses
    C. Ask someone else to do the job and rate him accordingly
    D. Ask for his reason for objecting to the request

10. As a supervisor of a small group of people, you have blamed worker A for something that you later find out was really done by worker B.
    The BEST thing for you to do now would be to
    A. say nothing to worker A but criticize worker B for his mistake while worker A is near so that A will realize that you know who made the mistake
    B. speak to each worker separately, apologize to worker A for your mistake, and discuss worker B's mistake with him
    C. bring both workers together, apologize to worker A for your mistake, and discuss worker B's mistake with him
    D. say nothing now but be careful about mixing up worker A with worker B in the future

11. You have just learned one of your staff is grumbling that she thinks you are not pleased with her work. As far as you're concerned, this isn't true at all. In fact, you've paid no particular attention to this worker lately because you've been very busy. You have just finished preparing an important report and *breaking in* a new clerk.
    Under the circumstances, the BEST thing to do is
    A. ignore her; after all, it's just a figment of her imagination
    B. discuss the matter with her now to try to find out and eliminate the cause of this problem
    C. tell her not to worry about it; you haven't had time to think about her work
    D. make a note to meet with her at a later date in order to straighten out the situation

12. A most important job of a supervisor is to positively motivate employees to increase their work production.
    Which of the following LEAST indicates that a group of workers has been positively motivated?
    A. Their work output becomes constant and stable.
    B. Their cooperation at work becomes greater.
    C. They begin to show pride in the product of their work.
    D. They show increased interest in their work

13. Which of the following traits would be LEAST important in considering a person for a merit increase?
    A. Punctuality   B. Using initiative successfully
    C. High rate of production   D. Resourcefulness

14. Of the following, the action LEAST likely to gain a supervisor the cooperation of his staff is for him to
    A. give each person consideration as an individual
    B. be as objective as possible when evaluating work performance
    C. rotate the least popular assignments
    D. expect subordinates to be equally competent

15. It has been said that, for the supervisor, nothing can beat the *face-to-face* communication of talking to one subordinate at a time.
This method is, however, LEAST appropriate to use when
    A. supervisor is explaining a change in general office procedure
    B. subject is of personal importance
    C. supervisor is conducting a yearly performance evaluation of all employees
    D. supervisor must talk to some of his employees concerning their poor attendance and punctuality

15._____

16. While you are on the telephone answering a question about your agency, a visitor comes to your desk and starts to ask you a question. There is no emergency or urgency in either situation, that of the phone call or that of answering the visitor's question.
In this case, you should
    A. continue to answer the person on the telephone until you are finished and then tell the visitor you are sorry to have kept him waiting
    B. excuse yourself to the person on the telephone and tell the visitor that you will be with him as soon as you have finished on the phone
    C. explain to the person on the telephone that you have a visitor and must shorten the conversation
    D. continue to answer the person on the phone while looking up occasionally at the visitor to let him know that you know he is waiting

16._____

17. While speaking on the telephone to someone who called, you are disconnected. The FIRST thing you should do is
    A. hang up but try to keep your line free to receive the call back
    B. immediately get the dial tone and continually dial the person who called you until you reach him
    C. signal the switchboard operator and ask her to re-establish the connection
    D. dial O for Operator and explain that you were disconnected

17._____

18. The type of speech used by an office worker in telephone conversations greatly affects the communicator.
Of the following, the BEST way to express your ideas when telephoning is with a vocabulary that consists mainly of _____ words.
    A. formal, intellectual sounding   B. often used colloquial
    C. technical, emphatic   D. simple, descriptive

18._____

19. Suppose a clerk under your supervision has taken a personal phone call and is at the same time needed to answer a question regarding an assignment being handled by another member of your office. He appears confused as to what he should do. How should you instruct him later as to how to handle a similar situation?
You should tell him to
    A. tell the caller to hold on while he answers the question
    B. tell the caller to call back a little later

19._____

C. return the call during an assigned break
D. finish the conversation quickly and answer the question

20. You are asked to place a telephone call by your supervisor. When you place the call, you receive what appears to be a wrong number.
Of the following, you should FIRST
    A. check the number with your supervisor to see if the number he gave you is correct
    B. ask the person on the other end what his number is and who he is
    C. check with the person on the other end to see if the number you dialed is the number you received
    D. apologize to the person on the other end for disturbing him and hang up

20._____

Questions 21-30.

DIRECTIONS: WORD MEANING
Each of Questions 21 through 30 contains a word in capitals followed by four suggested meanings of the word. For each question, choose the BEST meaning and write the letter of the best meaning in the space at the right.

21. ACCURATE
    A. correct   B. useful   C. afraid   D. careless

21._____

22. ALTER
    A. copy   B. change   C. repeat   D. agree

22._____

23. DOCUMENT
    A. outline   B. agreement   C. blueprint   D. record

23._____

24. INDICATE
    A. listen   B. show   C. guess   D. try

24._____

25. INVENTORY
    A. custom   B. discovery   C. warning   D. list

25._____

26. ISSUE
    A. annoy   B. use up   C. give out   D. gain

26._____

27. NOTIFY
    A. inform   B. promise   C. approve   D. strength

27._____

28. ROUTINE
    A. path   B. mistake   C. habit   D. journey

28._____

29. TERMINATE
    A. rest   B. start   C. deny   D. end

29._____

30. TRANSMIT
    A. put in   B. send   C. stop   D. go across

30._____

Questions 31-35.

DIRECTIONS: READING COMPREHENSION
Questions 31 through 35 test how well you understand what you read. It will be necessary for you to read carefully because your answers to these questions should be based SOLELY on the information given in the following paragraphs.

The recipient gains an impression of a typewritten letter before he begins to read the message. Factors which provide for a good first impression include margins and spacing that are visually pleasing, formal parts of the letter which are correctly placed according to the style of the letter, copy which is free of obvious erasures and over-strikes, and transcript that is even and clear. The problem for the typist is that of how to produce that first, positive impression of her work.

There are several general rules which a typist can follow when she wishes to prepare a properly spaced letter on a sheet of letterhead. Ordinarily, the width of a letter should not be less than four inches nor more than six inches. The side margins should also have a desirable relation to the bottom margin and the space between the letterhead and the body of the letter. Usually the most appealing arrangement is when the side margins are even and the bottom margin is slightly wider than the side margins. In some offices, however, standard line length is used for all business letters, and the secretary then varies the spacing between the date line and the inside address according to the length of the letter.

31. The BEST title for the above paragraphs would be
    A. Writing Office Letters
    B. Making Good First Impressions
    C. Judging Well-Typed Letters
    D. Good Placing and Spacing for Office Letters

31.____

32. According to the above paragraphs, which of the following might be considered the way in which people very quickly judge the quality of work which has been typed?
    By
    A. measuring the margins to see if they are correct
    B. looking at the spacing and cleanliness of the typescript
    C. scanning the body of the letter for meaning
    D. reading the date line and address for errors

32.____

33. What, according to the above paragraphs, would be definitely UNDESIRABLE as the average line length of a typed letter?
    A. 4"   B. 5"   C. 6"   D. 7"

33.____

34. According to the above paragraphs, when the line length is kept standard, the secretary
    A. does not have to vary the spacing at all since this also is standard
    B. adjusts the spacing between the date line and inside address for different lengths of letters
    C. uses the longest line as a guideline for spacing between the date line and inside address
    D. varies the number of spaces between the lines

34.____

7 (#1)

35. According to the above paragraphs, side margins are MOST pleasing when they 35._____
    A. are even and somewhat smaller than the bottom margin
    B. are slightly wider than the bottom margin
    C. vary with the length of the letter
    D. are figured independently from the letterhead and the body of the letter

Questions 36-40.

DIRECTIONS: CODING

        Name of Applicant   H A N G S B R U K E
        Test Code   c o m p l e x i t y
        File Number   0 1 2 3 4 5 6 7 8 9

Assume that each of the above capital letters is the first letter of the name of an applicant, that the small letter directly beneath each capital letter is the test code for the applicant, and that the number directly beneath each code letter is the file number for the applicant.

In each of the following Questions 36 through 40, the test code letters and the file numbers in Columns 2 and 3 should correspond to the capital letters in Column 1. For each question, look at each column carefully and mark your answer as follows:
    If there is an error only in Column 2, mark your answer A.
    If there is an error only in Column 3, mark your answer B.
    If there is an error in both Columns 2 and 3, mark your answer C.
    If both Columns 2 and 3 are correct, mark your answer D.

The following sample question is given to help you understand the procedure.

SAMPLE QUESTION

Column 1	Column 2	Column 3
AKEHN	otyci	18902

In Column 2, the final test code letter *i* should be *m*. Column 3 is correctly coded in Column 1. Since there is an error only in Column 2, the answer is A.

	Column 1	Column 2	Column 3	
36.	NEKKU	mytti	29987	36._____
37.	KRAEB	txlye	86095	37._____
38.	ENAUK	ymoit	92178	38._____
39.	REANA	xeomo	69121	39._____
40.	EKHSE	ytcxy	97049	

Questions 41-50.

DIRECTIONS: ARITHMETICAL REASONING
Solve the following problems.

41. If a secretary answered 28 phone calls and typed the addresses for 112 credit statements in one morning, what is the RATIO of phone calls answered to credit statements typed for that period of time?
   A. 1:4   B. 1:7   C. 2:3   D. 3:5

42. According to a suggested filing system, no more than 10 folders should be filed behind any one file guide, and from 15 to 25 file guides should be used in each file drawer for easy finding and filing.
The MAXIMUM number of folders that a five-drawer file cabinet can hold to allow easy finding and filing is
   A. 550   B. 750   C. 1,100   D. 1,250

43. An employee had a starting salary of $32,902. He received a salary increase at the end of each year, and at the end of the seventh year, his salary was $36,738.
What was his AVERAGE annual increase in salary over these seven years?
   A. $510   B. $538   C. $548   D. $572

44. The 55 typists and 28 senior clerks in a certain agency were paid a total of $1,943,200 in salaries for the year.
If the average annual salary of a typist was $22,400, the average annual salary of a senior clerk was
   A. $25,400   B. $26,600   C. $26,800   D. $27,000

45. A typist has been given a three-page report to type. She has finished typing the first two pages. The first page has 283 words, and the second page has 366 words.
If the total report consists of 954 words, how many words will she have to type on the third page of the report?
   A. 202   B. 287   C. 305   D. 313

46. In one day, Clerk A processed 30% more forms than Clerk B, and Clerk C processed 11/4 as many forms as Clerk A.
If Clerk B processed 40 forms, how many MORE forms were processed by Clerk C?
   A. 12   B. 13   C. 21   D. 25

47. A clerk who earns a gross salary of $452 every week has the following deductions taken from her paycheck: 17½% for City, State, Federal taxes, and for Social Security, $1.20 for health insurance, and $6.10 for union dues.
The amount of her take-home pay is
   A. $286.40   B. $312.40   C. $331.60   D. $365.60

48. In 2022 an agency spent $400 to buy pencils at a cost of $1 a dozen. If the agency used ¾ of these pencils in 2022 and used the same number of pencils in 2023, how many MORE pencils did it have to buy to have enough pencils for all of 2023?
    A. 1,200   B. 2,400   C. 3,600   D. 4,800

49. A clerk who worked in Agency X earned the following salaries: $30,070 the first year, $30,500 the second year, and $30,960 the third year. Another clerk who worked in Agency Y for three years earned $30,550 a year for two years and $30,724 the third year.
    The DIFFERENCE between the average salaries received by both clerks over a three-year period is
    A. $98   B. $102   C. $174   D. $282

50. An employee who works over 40 hours in any week receives overtime payment for the extra hours at time and one-half (1½ times) his hourly rate of pay. An employee who earns $15.60 an hour works a total of 45 hours during a certain week.
    His TOTAL pay for that week would be
    A. $624.00   B. $702.00   C. $741.00   D. $824.00

KEY (CORRECT ANSWERS)

1.	B	11.	B	21.	A	31.	D	41.	A
2.	C	12.	A	22.	B	32.	B	42.	D
3.	D	13.	A	23.	D	33.	D	43.	C
4.	C	14.	D	24.	B	34.	B	44.	A
5.	D	15.	A	25.	D	35.	A	45.	C
6.	C	16.	B	26.	C	36.	B	46.	D
7.	A	17.	A	27.	A	37.	C	47.	D
8.	D	18.	D	28.	C	38.	D	48.	B
9.	D	19.	C	29.	D	39.	A	49.	A
10.	B	20.	C	30.	B	40.	C	50.	C

TEST 2

DIRECTIONS: Each question or incomplete statement is followed by several suggested answers or completions. Select the one that BEST answers the question or completes the statement. *PRINT THE LETTER OF THE CORRECT ANSWER IN THE SPACE AT THE RIGHT.*

1. To tell a newly employed clerk to fill a top drawer of a four-drawer cabinet with heavy folders which will be often used and to keep lower drawers only partly filled is
    A. *good*, because a tall person would have to bend unnecessarily if he had to use a lower drawer
    B. *bad*, because the file cabinet may tip over when the top drawer is opened
    C. *good*, because it is the most easily reachable drawer for the average person
    D. *bad*, because a person bending down at another drawer may accidentally bang his head on the bottom of the drawer when he straightens up

2. If you have requisitioned a ream of paper in order to duplicate a single page office announcement, how many announcements can be printed from the one package of paper?
    A. 200   B. 500   C. 700   D. 1,000

3. In the operations of a government agency, a voucher is ORDINARILY used to
    A. refer someone to the agency for a position or assignment
    B. certify that an agency's records of financial transactions are accurate
    C. order payment from agency funds of a stated amount to an individual
    D. enter a statement of official opinion in the records of the agency

4. Of the following types of cards used in filing systems, the one which is generally MOST helpful in locating records which might be filed under more than one subject is the _____ card.
    A. cut
    B. tickler
    C. cross-reference
    D. visible index

5. The type of filing system in which one does NOT need to refer to a card index in order to find the folder is called
    A. alphabetic   B. geographic   C. subject   D. locational

6. Of the following, records management is LEAST concerned with
    A. the development of the best method for retrieving important information
    B. deciding what records should be kept
    C. deciding the number of appointments a client will need
    D. determining the types of folders to be used

7. If records are continually removed from a set of files without *charging* them to the borrower, the filing system will soon become ineffective.
   Of the following terms, the one which is NOT applied to a form used in a charge-out system is a
   A. requisition card
   B. out-folder
   C. record retrieval form
   D. substitution card

8. A new clerk has been told to put 500 cards in alphabetical order. Another clerk suggests that she divide the cards into four groups such as A to F, G to L, M to R, and S to Z, and then alphabetize these four smaller groups.
   The suggested method is
   A. *poor*, because the clerk will have to handle the sheets more than once and will waste time
   B. *good*, because it saves time, is more accurate, and is less tiring
   C. *good*, because she will not have to concentrate on it so much when it is in smaller groups
   D. *bad*, because this method is much more tiring than straight alphabetizing

9. The term that describes the equipment attached to an office computer is
   A. interface   B. network   C. hardware   D. software

10. Suppose a clerk has been given pads of pre-printed forms to use when taking phone messages for others in her office. The clerk is then observed using scraps of paper and not the forms for writing her messages.
    It should be explained that the BEST reason for using the forms is that
    A. they act as a checklist to make sure that the important information is taken
    B. she is expected to do her work in the same way as others in the office
    C. they make sure that unassigned paper is not wasted on phone messages
    D. learning to use these forms will help train her to use more difficult forms

11. Of the following, the one which is spelled INCORRECTLY is
    A. alphabetization
    B. reccommendation
    C. redaction
    D. synergy

12. Of the following, the MAIN reason a stock clerk keeps a perpetual inventory of supplies in the storeroom is that such an inventory will
    A. eliminate the need for a physical inventory
    B. provide a continuous record of supplies on hand
    C. indicate whether a shipment of supplies is satisfactory
    D. dictate the terms of the purchase order

13. As a supervisor, you may be required to handle different types of correspondence.
    Of the following types of letters, it would be MOST important to promptly seal which kind of letters?

A. One marked *confidential*
B. Those containing enclosures
C. Any letter to be sent airmail
D. Those in which carbons will be sent along with the original

14. While opening incoming mail, you notice that one letter indicates that an enclosure was to be included but, even after careful inspection,, you are not able to find the information to which this refers.
Of the following, the thing that you should do FIRST is
   A. replace the letter in its envelope and return it to the sender
   B. file the letter until the sender's office mails the missing information
   C. type out a letter to the sender informing them of their error
   D. make a notation in the margin of the letter that the enclosure was omitted

14.____

15. You have been given a checklist and assigned the responsibility of inspecting certain equipment in the various offices of your agency.
Which of the following is the GREATEST advantage of the checklist?
   A. It indicates which equipment is in greatest demand.
   B. Each piece of equipment on the checklist will be checked only once.
   C. It helps to insure that the equipment listed will not be overlooked.
   D. The equipment listed suggests other equipment you should look for.

15.____

16. Your supervisor has asked you to locate a telephone number for an attorney named Jones, whose office is located at 311 Broadway and whose name is not already listed in your files.
The BEST method for finding the number would be for you to
   A. call the information operator and have her get it for you
   B. look in the alphabetical directory (white pages) under the name Jones at 311 Broadway
   C. refer to the heading Attorney in the yellow pages for the name Jones at 311 Broadway
   D. ask your supervisor who referred her to Mr. Jones, then call that person for the number

16.____

17. An example of material that should NOT be sent by first class mail is a
   A. carbon copy of a letter   B. postcard
   C. business reply card   D. large catalogue

17.____

18. Which of the following BEST describes *office work simplification*?
   A. An attempt to increase the rate of production by speeding up the movements of employees
   B. Eliminating wasteful steps in order to increase efficiency
   C. Making jobs as easy as possible for employees so they will not be overworked
   D. Eliminating all difficult tasks from an office and leaving only simple ones

18.____

19. The duties of a supervisor who is assigned the job of timekeeper may include all of the following EXCEPT
    A. computing and recording regular hours worked each day in accordance with the normal work schedule
    B. approving requests for vacation leave, sick leave, and annual leave
    C. computing and recording overtime hours worked beyond the normal schedule
    D. determining the total regular hours and total extra hours worked during the week

19.____

20. Suppose a clerk under your supervision accidentally opens a personal letter while handling office mail.
    Under such circumstances, you should tell the clerk to put the letter back in the envelope and
    A. take the letter to the person to whom it belongs and make sure he understands that the clerk did not read it
    B. try to seal the envelope so it won't appear to have been opened
    C. write on the envelope *Sorry, opened by mistake*, and put his initials on it
    D. write on the envelope *Sorry, opened by mistake*, but not put his initials on it

20.____

Questions 21-25.

DIRECTIONS: SPELLING
Each Question 21 through 25 consists of three words. In each question, one of the words may be spelled incorrectly or all three may be spelled correctly. For each question, if one of the words is spelled incorrectly, write the letter of the incorrect word in the space at the right. If all three words are spelled correctly, write the letter D in the space at the right.

SAMPLE I: (A) guide (B) departmint (C) stranger
SAMPLE II: (A) comply (B) valuable (C) window

In Sample Question I, *departmint* is incorrect. It should be spelled *department*. Therefore, B is the answer to Sample Question 1.
In Sample Question II, all three words are spelled correctly. Therefore D is the answer to Sample Question II.

21.	A. argument	B. reciept	C. complain	21.____
22.	A. sufficient	B. postpone	C. visible	22.____
23.	A. expirience	B. dissatisfy	C. alternate	23.____
24.	A. occurred	B. noticable	C. appendix	24.____
25.	A. anxious	B. guarantee	C. calender	25.____

Questions 26-30.

DIRECTIONS: ENGLISH USAGE
Each Question 26 through 30 contains a sentence. Read each sentence carefully to decide whether it is correct. Then, in the space at the right, mark your answer:
A. if the sentence is incorrect because of bad grammar or sentence structure
B. of the sentence is incorrect because of bad punctuation
C. if the sentence is incorrect because of bad capitalization
D. if the sentence is correct

Each incorrect sentence has only one type of error. Consider a sentence correct if it has no errors, although there may be other correct ways of saying the same thing.

SAMPLE QUESTION I: One of our clerks were promoted yesterday.
The subject of this sentence is *one*, so the verb should be *was promoted* instead of *were promoted*. Since the sentence is incorrect because of bad grammar, the answer to Sample Question I is A.

SAMPLE QUESTION II: Between you and me, I would prefer not going there.
Since this sentence is correct, the answer to Sample Question II is D.

26. The National alliance of Businessmen is trying to persuade private businesses to hire youth in the summertime. 26.____

27. The supervisor who is on vacation, is in charge of processing vouchers. 27.____

28. The activity of the committee at its conferences is always stimulating. 28.____

29. After checking the addresses again, the letters went to the mailroom. 29.____

30. The director, as well as the employees, are interested in sharing the dividends. 30.____

Questions 31-40.

DIRECTIONS: FILING
Each Question 31 through 40 contains four names. For each question, choose the name that should be FIRST if the four names are to be arranged in alphabetical order in accordance with the Rules for Alphabetical Filing given below. Read these rules carefully. Then, for each question, indicate in the correspondingly numbered space at the right the letter before the name that should be FIRST in alphabetical order.

RULES FOR ALPHABETICAL FILING

Names of People

1. The names of people are filed in strict alphabetical order, first according to the last name, then according to first name or initial, and finally according to middle name or initial. For example: George Allen comes before Edward Bell, and Leonard P. Reston comes before Lucille B. Reston.

2. When last names are the same, for example A. Green and Agnes Green, the one with the initial comes before the one with the name written out when the first initials are identical.

3. When first and last names are alike and the middle initial is given, for example John David Doe and John Devoe Doe, the names should be filed in the alphabetical order of the middle names.

4. When first and last names are the same, a name without a middle initial comes before one with a middle name or initial. For example, John Doe comes before both John A. Doe and John Alan Doe.

5. When first and last names are the same, a name with a middle initial comes before one with a middle name beginning with the same initial. For example: Jack R. Herts comes before Jack Richard Hertz.

6. Prefixes such as De, O', Mac, Mc, and Van are filed as written and are treated as part of the names to which they are connected. For example: Robert O'Dea is filed before David Olsen.

7. Abbreviated names are treated as if they were spelled out. For example: Chas. is filed as Charles and Thos. is filed as Thomas.

8. Titles and designations such as Dr., Mr., and Prof. are disregarded in filing.

Names of Organizations

1. The names of business organizations are filed according to the order in which each word in the name appears. When an organization name bears the name of a person, it is filed according to the rules for filing names of people as given above. For example, William Smith Service Co. comes before Television Distributors, Inc.

2. Where bureau, board, office or department appears as the first part of the title of a governmental agency, that agency should be filed under the word in the title expressing the chief function of the agency. For example: Bureau of the Budget would be filed as if written Budget, (Bureau of the). The Department of Personnel would be filed as if written Personnel (Department of).

3. When the following words are part of an organization, they are disregarded: the, of, and.

7 (#2)

4. When there are numbers in a name, they are treated as if they were spelled out. For example: 10th Street Bootery is filed as Tenth Street Bootery.

SAMPLE QUESTION: A. Jane Earl   (2)
                  B. James A. Earle   (4)
                  C. James Earl   (1)
                  D. J. Earle   (3)

The numbers in parentheses show the proper alphabetical order in which these names should be filed. Since the name that should be filed FIRST is James Earl, the answer to the sample question is C.

31. A. Majorca Leather Goods   B. Robert Majorca and Sons   31._____
    C. Maintenance Management Corp.   D. Majestic Carpet Mills

32. A. Municipal Telephone Service   B. Municipal Reference Library   32._____
    C. Municipal Credit Union   D. Municipal Broadcasting System

33. A. Robert B. Pierce   B. R. Bruce Pierce   33._____
    C. Ronald Pierce   D. Robert Bruce Pierce

34. A. Four Seasons Sports Club   B. 14 Street Shopping Center   34._____
    C. Forty Thieves Restaurant   D. 42nd St. Theaters

35. A. Franco Franceschini   B. Amos Franchini   35._____
    C. Sandra Franceschia   D. Lilie Franchinesca

36. A. Chas. A. Levine   B. Kurt Levene   36._____
    C. Charles Levine   D. Kurt E. Levene

37. A. Prof. Geo. Kinkaid   B. Mr. Alan Kinkaid   37._____
    C. Dr. Albert A. Kinkade   D. Kincade Liquors Inc.

38. A. Department of Public Events   B. Office of the Public Administrator   38._____
    C. Queensborough Public Library   D. Department of Public Health

39. A. Martin Luther King, Jr. Towers B. Metro North Plaza   39._____
    C. Manhattanville Houses   D. Marble Hill Houses

40. A. Dr. Arthur Davids   B. The David Check Cashing Service 40._____
    C. A.C. Davidsen   D. Milton Davidoff

Questions 41-45.

DIRECTIONS: READING COMPREHENSION
Questions 41 through 45 test how well you understand what you read. It will be necessary for you to read carefully because your answers to these questions should be based SOLELY on the information given in the following paragraph.

Work standards presuppose an ability to measure work. Measurement in office management is needed for several reasons. First, it is necessary to evaluate the overall efficiency of the office itself. It is then essential to measure the efficiency of each particular section or unit and that of the individual worker. To plan and control the work of sections and units, one must have measurement. A program of measurement goes hand in hand with a program of standards. One can have measurement without standards, but one cannot have work standards without measurement. Providing data on amount of work done and time expended, measurement does not deal with the amount of energy expended by an individual although in many cases such energy may be in direct proportion to work output. Usually from two-thirds to three fourths of all work can be measured. However, less than two-thirds of all work is actually measured because measurement difficulties are encountered when office work is non-repetitive and irregular, or when it is primarily mental rather than manual. These obstacles are often used as excuses for non-measurement far more frequently than is justified.

41. According to the paragraph, an office manager cannot set work standards unless he can
    A. plan the amount of work to be done
    B. control the amount of work that is done
    C. estimate accurately the quantity of work done
    D. delegate the amount of work to be done to efficient workers

42. According to the paragraph, the type of office work that would be MOST difficult to measure would be
    A. checking warrants for accuracy of information
    B. recording payroll changes
    C. processing applications
    D. making up a new system of giving out supplies

43. According to the paragraph, the actual amount of work that is measured is _____ of all work.
    A. less than two-thirds
    B. two-thirds to three-fourths
    C. less than three-sixths
    D. more than three-fourths

44. Which of the following would be MOST difficult to determine by using measurement techniques?
    A. The amount of work that is accomplished during a certain period of time
    B. The amount of work that should be planned for a period of time
    C. How much time is needed to do a certain task
    D. The amount of incentive a person must have to do his job

45. The one of the following which is the MOST suitable title for the paragraph is:
    A. How Measurement of Office Efficiency Depends on Work Standards
    B. Using Measurement for Office Management and Efficiency
    C. Work Standards and the Efficiency of the Office Worker
    D. Managing the Office Using Measured Work Standards

Questions 46-50.

DIRECTIONS: INTERPRETING STATISTICAL DATA
Questions 46 through 50 are to be answered using the information given in the following table.

AGE COMPOSITION IN THE LABOR FORCE IN CITY A
(2010-2020)

	Age Group	2010	2015	2020
Men	14-24	8,430	10,900	14,340
	25-44	22,200	22,350	26,065
	45+	17,550	19,800	21,970
Women	14-24	4,450	6,915	7,680
	25-44	9,080	10,010	11,550
	45+	7,325	9,470	13,180

46. The GREATEST increase in the number of people in the labor force between 2010 and 2015 occurred among
    A. men between the ages of 14 and 24
    B. men age 45 and over
    C. women between the ages of 14 and 24
    D. women age 45 and over

47. If the total number of women of all ages in the labor force increases from 2020 to 2025 by the same number as it did from 2015 to 2020, the TOTAL number of women of all ages in the labor force in 2025 will be
    A. 27,425   B. 29,675   C. 37,525   D. 38,425

48. The total increase in number of women in the labor force from 2010 to 2015 differs from the total increase of men in the same years by being _____ than that of men.
    A. 770 less   B. 670 more   C. 770 more   D. 1,670 more

49. In the year 2010, the proportion of married women in each group was as follows: 1/5 of the women in the 14-24 age group, 1/4 of those in the 25-44 age group, and 2/5 of those 45 and over.
    How many married women were in the labor force in 2010?
    A. 4,625   B. 5,990   C. 6,090   D. 7,910

50. The 14-24 age group of men in the labor force from 2010 to 2020 increased by APPROXIMATELY
    A. 40%   B. 65%   C. 70%   D. 75%

KEY (CORRECT ANSWERS)

1. B	11. B	21. B	31. C	41. C
2. B	12. B	22. D	32. D	42. D
3. C	13. A	23. A	33. B	43. A
4. C	14. D	24. B	34. D	44. D
5. A	15. C	25. C	35. C	45. B
6. C	16. C	26. C	36. B	46. A
7. C	17. D	27. B	37. D	47. D
8. B	18. B	28. D	38. B	48. B
9. C	19. B	29. A	39. A	49. C
10. A	20. C	30. A	40. B	50. C

EXAMINATION SECTION
TEST 1

DIRECTIONS: Each question or incomplete statement is followed by several suggested answers or completions. Select the one that BEST answers the question or completes the statement. *PRINT THE LETTER OF THE CORRECT ANSWER IN THE SPACE AT THE RIGHT.*

Questions 1-4.

DIRECTIONS: Questions 1 through 4 are to be answered SOLELY on the basis of the following passage.

Job analysis combined with performance appraisal is an excellent method of determining training needs of individuals. The steps in this method are to determine the specific duties of the job, to evaluate the adequacy with which the employee performs each of these duties, and finally to determine what significant improvements can be made by training.

The list of duties can be obtained in a number of ways: asking the employee, asking the supervisor, observing the employee, etc. Adequacy of performance can be estimated by the employee, but the supervisor's evaluation must also be obtained. This evaluation will usually be based on observation.

What does the supervisor observe? The employee, while he is working; the employee's work relationships; the ease, speed, and sureness of the employee's actions; the way he applies himself to the job; the accuracy and amount of completed work; its conformity with established procedures and standards; the appearance of the work; the soundness of judgment it shows; and, finally, signs of good or poor communication, understanding, and cooperation among employees.

Such observation is a normal and inseparable part of the everyday job of supervision. Systematically, recorded, evaluated, and summarized, it highlights both general and individual training needs.

1. According to the passage, job analysis may be used by the supervisor in   1.____
   A. increasing his own understanding of tasks performed in his unit
   B. increasing efficiency of communication within the organization
   C. assisting personnel experts in the classification of positions
   D. determining in which areas an employee needs more instruction

2. According to the passage, the FIRST step in determining the training needs of   2.____
   employees is to
   A. locate the significant improvements that can be made by training
   B. determine the specific duties required in a job
   C. evaluate the employee's performance
   D. motivate the employee to want to improve himself

3. On the basis of the above passage, which of the following is the BEST way for a supervisor to determine the adequacy of employee performance?
   A. Check the accuracy and amount of completed work
   B. Ask the training officer
   C. Observe all aspects of the employee's work
   D. Obtain the employee's own estimate

4. Which of the following is NOT mentioned by the passage as a factor to be taken into consideration in judging the adequacy of employee performance?
   A. Accuracy of completed work
   B. Appearance of completed work
   C. Cooperation among employees
   D. Attitude of the employee toward his supervisor

5. In indexing names of business firms and other organizations, ONE of the rules to be followed is:
   A. The word *and* is considered an indexing unit.
   B. When a firm name includes the full name of a person who is not well-known, the person's first name is considered as the first indexing unit.
   C. Usually the units in a firm name are indexed in the order in which they are written.
   D. When a firm's name is made up of single letters (such as ABC Corp.), the letters taken together are considered more than one indexing unit.

6. Assume that people often come to your office with complaints of errors in your agency's handling of their clients. The employees in your office have the job of listening to these complaints and investigating them. One day, when it is almost closing time, a person comes into your office, apparently very angry, and demands that you take care of his complaint at once.
   Your IMMEDIATE reaction should be to
   A. suggest that he return the following day
   B. find out his name and the nature of his complaint
   C. tell him to write a letter
   D. call over your supervisor

7. Assume that part of your job is to notify people concerning whether their applications for a certain program have been approved or disapproved. However, you do not actually make the decision on approval or disapproval. One day, you answer a telephone call from a woman who states that she has not yet received any word on her application. She goes on to tell you her qualifications for the program. From what she has said, you know that persons with such qualifications are usually approved.
   Of the following, which one is the BEST thing for you to say to her?
   A. "You probably will be accepted, but wait until you receive a letter before trying to join the program."
   B. "Since you seem well qualified, I am sure that your application will be approved."

C. "If you can write us a letter emphasizing your qualifications, it may speed up the process."
D. "You will be notified of the results of your application as soon as a decision has been made."

8. Suppose that one of your duties includes answering specific telephone inquiries. Your superior refers a call to you from an irate person who claims that your agency is inefficient and is wasting taxpayers' money.
Of the following, the BEST way to handle such a call is to
   A. listen briefly and then hang up without answering
   B. note the caller's comments and tell him that you will transmit them to your superiors
   C. connect the caller with the head of your agency
   D. discuss your own opinions with the caller

8._____

9. An employee has been assigned to open her division head's mail and place it on his desk. One day, the employee opens a letter which she then notices is marked *Personal*.
Of the following, the BEST action for her to take is to
   A. write *Personal* on the letter and staple the envelope to the back of the letter
   B. ignore the matter and treat the letter the same way as the others
   C. give it to another division head to hold until her own division head comes into the office
   D. leave the letter in the envelope and write *Sorry opened by mistake* on the envelope and initial it

9._____

Questions 10-14.

DIRECTIONS: Questions 10 through 14 each consist of a quotation which contains one word that is incorrectly used because it is not in keeping with the meaning that the quotation is evidently intended to convey. Of the words underlined in each quotation, determine which word is incorrectly used. Then select from among the words lettered A, B, C, and D the word which, when substituted for the incorrectly used word, would BEST help to convey the meaning of the quotation. (Do not indicate a change for an underlined word unless the underlined word is incorrectly used.)

10. Unless reasonable managerial supervision is <u>exercised</u> over office supplies, it is certain that there will be extravagance, <u>rejected</u> items out of stock, <u>excessive</u> prices paid for certain items, and <u>obsolete</u> material in the stockroom.
    A. overlooked   B. immoderate   C. needed   D. instituted

10._____

11. Since <u>office</u> supplies are in such <u>common</u> use, an attitude of indifference about their handling is not <u>unusual</u>. Their importance is often recognized only when they are <u>utilized</u> or out of stock, for office employees must have proper supplies if maximum productivity is to be <u>attained</u>.
    A. plentiful   B. unavailable   C. reduced   D. expected

11._____

12. Anyone effected by paperwork, interested in or engaged in office work, or desiring to improve informational activities can find materials keyed to his needs.
    A. attentive   B. available   C. affected   D. ambitious

13. Information is homogeneous and must therefore be properly classified so that each type may be employed in ways appropriate to its own peculiar properties.
    A. apparent   B. heterogeneous
    C. consistent   D. idiosyncratic

14. Intellectual training may seem a formidable phrase, but it means nothing more than the deliberate cultivation of the ability to think, and there is no dark contrast between the intellectual and the practical.
    A. subjective   B. objective   C. sharp   D. vocational

15. The MOST important reason for having a filing system is to
    A. get papers out of the way
    B. have a record of everything that has happened
    C. retain information to justify your actions
    D. enable rapid retrieval of information

16. The system of filing which is used MOST frequently is called _____ filing.
    A. alphabetic   B. alphanumeric
    C. geographic   D. numeric

17. One of the clerks under your supervision has been telephoning frequently to tell you that he was taking the day off. Unless there is a real need for it, taking leave which is not scheduled is frowned upon because it upsets the work schedule.
    Under these circumstances, which of the following reasons for taking the day off is MOST acceptable?
    A. "I can't work when my arthritis bothers me."
    B. "I've been pressured with work from my night job and needed the extra time to catch up."
    C. "My family just moved to a new house, and I needed the time to start the repairs."
    D. "Work here has not been challenging, and I've been looking for another job."

18. One of the employees under your supervision, previously a very satisfactory worker, has begun arriving late one or two mornings each week. No explanation has been offered for this change. You call her to your office for a conference. As you are explaining the purpose of the conference and your need to understand this sudden lateness problem, she becomes very angry and states that you have no right to question her.
    Of the following, the BEST course of action for you to take at this point is to

A. inform her in your most authoritarian tone that you are the supervisor and that you have every right to question her
B. end the conference and advise the employee that you will have no further discussion with her until she controls her temper
C. remain calm, try to calm her down, and when she has quieted, explain the reasons for your questions and the need for answers
D. hold your temper; when she has calmed down, tell her that you will not have a tardy worker in your unit and will have her transferred at once

19. Assume that, in the branch of the agency for which you work, you are the only clerical person on the staff with a supervisory title and, in addition, that you are the office manager. On a particular day when all members of the professional staff are away from the building attending an important meeting, an urgent call comes through requesting some confidential information ordinarily released only by professional staff.
Of the following, the MOST reasonable action for you to take is to
    A. decline to give the information because you are not a member of the professional staff
    B. offer to call back after you get permission from the agency director at the main office
    C. advise the caller that you will supply the information as soon as your chief returns
    D. supply the information requested and inform your chief when she returns

19._____

20. As a supervisor, you are scheduled to attend an important conference with your superior. However, that day you learn that your very capable assistant is ill and unable to come to work. Several highly sensitive tasks are scheduled for completion on this day.
Of the following, the BEST way to handle this situation is to
    A. tell your supervisor you cannot attend the meeting and ask that it be postponed
    B. assign one of your staff to see that the jobs are completed and turned in
    C. advise your supervisor of the situation and ask what you should do
    D. call the departments for which the work is being done and ask for an extension of time

20._____

21. When a decision needs to be made which is likely to affect units other than his own, a supervisor should USUALLY
    A. make such a decision quickly and then discuss it with his supervisor
    B. make such a decision only after careful consultation with his subordinates
    C. discuss the problem with his immediate superior before making such a decision
    D. have his subordinates arrive at such a decision in conference with the subordinates in the other units

21._____

22. Assume that, as a supervisor in Division X, you are training Ms. Y, a new employee, to answer the telephone properly.
You should explain that the BEST way to answer is to pick up the receiver and say:

22._____

A. "What is your name, please?" B. "May I help you?"
C. "Ms. Y speaking." D. "Division X, Ms. Y speaking."

Questions 23-25.

DIRECTIONS: Questions 23 through 25 consist of sentences in which two words are missing. Examine each sentence, and then choose from below it the words which should be inserted in the blank spaces in order to create a coherent and well-written sentence.

23. Human behavior is far _____ variable, and therefore _____ predictable, than that of any other species.   23.____
    A. less; as   B. less; not   C. more; not   D. more; less

24. The _____ limitation of this method is that the results are based _____ a narrow sample.   24.____
    A. chief; with   B. chief; on   C. only; for   D. only; to

25. Although there _____ a standard procedure for handling these problems, each case often has _____ own unique features.   25.____
    A. are; its   B. are; their   C. is; its   D. is; their

KEY (CORRECT ANSWERS)

1.	D		11.	B
2.	B		12.	C
3.	C		13.	B
4.	D		14.	C
5.	C		15.	D
6.	B		16.	A
7.	D		17.	A
8.	B		18.	C
9.	D		19.	B
10.	C		20.	C

21. C
22. D
23. D
24. B
25. C

TEST 2

DIRECTIONS: Each question or incomplete statement is followed by several suggested answers or completions. Select the one that BEST answers the question or completes the statement. *PRINT THE LETTER OF THE CORRECT ANSWER IN THE SPACE AT THE RIGHT.*

Questions 1-3.

DIRECTIONS: Questions 1 through 3 each consist of a group of four sentences. Read each sentence carefully, and select the one of the four in each group which represents the BEST English usage for business letters and reports.

1. A. The chairman himself, rather than his aides, has reviewed the report.
   B. The chairman himself, rather than his aides, have reviewed the report.
   C. The chairmen, not the aide, has reviewed the report.
   D. The aide, not the chairmen, have reviewed the report.

   1.____

2. A. Various proposals were submitted but the decision is not been made.
   B. Various proposals has been submitted but the decision has not been made.
   C. Various proposals were submitted but the decision is not been made.
   D. Various proposals have been submitted but the decision has not been made.

   2.____

3. A. Everyone were rewarded for his successful attempt.
   B. They were successful in their attempts and each of them was rewarded.
   C. Each of them are rewarded for their successful attempts.
   D. The reward for their successful attempts were made to each of them.

   3.____

4. Which of the following is MOST suited to arrangement in chronological order?
   A. Applications for various types and levels of jobs
   B. Issues of a weekly publication
   C. Weekly time cards for all employees for the week of April 21
   D. Personnel records for all employees

   4.____

5. Words that are *synonymous* with a given word ALWAYS _____ the given word.
   A. have the same meaning as
   B. have the same pronunciation as
   C. have the opposite meaning of
   D. can be rhymed with

   5.____

Questions 6-11.

DIRECTIONS: Questions 6 through 11 are to be answered on the basis of the following chart showing numbers of errors made by four clerks in one work unit for a half-year period.

49

2 (#2)

	Allan	Barry	Cary	David
July	5	4	1	7
August	8	3	9	8
September	7	8	7	5
October	3	6	5	3
November	2	4	4	6
December	5	2	8	4

6. The clerk with the HIGHEST number of errors for the six-month period was
   A. Allan B. Barry C. Cary D. David

7. If the number of errors made by Allan in the six months shown represented one-eighth of the total errors made by the unit during the entire year, what was the TOTAL number of errors made by the unit for the year?
   A. 124 B. 180 C. 240 D. 360

8. The number of errors made by David in November was what FRACTION of the total errors made in November?
   A. 1/3 B. 1/6 C. 3/8 D. 3/16

9. The average number of errors made per month per clerk was MOST NEARLY
   A. 4 B. 5 C. 6 D. 7

10. Of the total number of errors made during the six-month period, the percentage made in August was MOST NEARLY
    A. 2% B. 4% C. 23% D. 4%

11. If the number of errors in the unit were to decrease in the next six months by 30%, what would be MOST NEARLY the total number of errors for the unit for the next six months?
    A. 87 B. 94 C. 120 D. 137

12. The arithmetic mean salary for five employees earning $18,500, $18,300, $18,600, $18,400, and $18,500, respectively is
    A. $18,450 B. $18,460 C. $18,475 D. $18,500

13. Last year, a city department which is responsible for purchasing supplies ordered bond paper in equal quantities from 22 different companies. The price was exactly the same for each company, and the total cost for the 22 orders was $693,113.
    Assuming prices did not change during the year, the cost of EACH order was MOST NEARLY
    A. $31,490 B. $31,495 C. $31,500 D. $31,505

14. A city agency engaged in repair work uses a small part which the city purchases for $0.14 each. Assume that, in a certain year, the total expenditure of the city for this part was $700.
How MANY of these parts were purchased that year?
A. 50 B. 200 C. 2,000 D. 5,000

15. The work unit which you supervise is responsible for processing fifteen reports per month.
If your unit has four clerks and the best worker completes 40% of the reports himself, how many reports would each of the other clerks have to complete if they all do an equal number?
A. 1 B. 2 C. 3 D. 4

16. Assume that the work unit in which you work has 24 clerks and 18 stenographers. In order to change the ratio of stenographers to clerks so that there is one stenographer for every four clerks, it would be necessary to REDUCE the number of stenographers by
A. 3 B. 6 C. 9 D. 12

17. Assume that your office is responsible for opening and distributing all the mail of the division. After opening a letter, one of your subordinates notices that it states that there should be an enclosure in the envelope. However, there is no enclosure in the envelope.
Of the following, the BEST instruction that you can give the clerk is to
A. call the sender to obtain the enclosure
B. call the addressee to inform him that the enclosure is missing
C. note the omission in the margin of the letter
D. forward the letter without taking any action

18. While opening the envelope containing official correspondence, you accidentally cut the enclosed letter.
Of the following, the BEST action for you to take is to
A. leave the material as it is
B. put it together by using transparent mending tape
C. keep it together by putting it back in the envelope
D. keep it together by using paper clips

19. Suppose your supervisor is on the telephone in his office and an applicant arrives for a scheduled interview with him.
Of the following, the BEST procedure to follow ordinarily is to
A. informally chat with the applicant in your office until your supervisor has finished his phone conversation
B. escort him directly into your supervisor's office and have him wait for him there
C. inform your supervisor of the applicant's arrival and try to make the applicant feel comfortable while waiting
D. have him hang up his coat and tell him to go directly in to see your supervisor

20. The length of time that files should be kept is GENERALLY
    A. considered to be seven years
    B. dependent upon how much new material has accumulated in the files
    C. directly proportionate to the number of years the office has been in operation
    D. dependent upon the type and nature of the material in the files

21. Cross-referencing a document when you file it means
    A. making a copy of the document and putting the copy into a related file
    B. indicating on the front of the document the name of the person who wrote it, the date it was written, and for what purpose
    C. putting a special sheet or card in a related file to indicate where the document is filed
    D. indicating on the document where it is to be filed

22. Unnecessary handling and recording of incoming mail could be eliminated by
    A. having the person who opens it initial it
    B. indicating on the piece of mail the names of all the individuals who should see it
    C. sending all incoming mail to more than one central location
    D. making a photocopy of each piece of incoming mail

23. Of the following, the office tasks which lend themselves MOST readily to planning and study are
    A. repetitive, occur in volume, and extend over a period of time
    B. cyclical in nature, have small volume, and extend over a short period of time
    C. tasks which occur only once in a great while not according to any schedule, and have large volume
    D. special tasks which occur only once, regardless of their volume and length of time

24. A good recordkeeping system includes all of the following procedures EXCEPT the
    A. filing of useless records
    B. destruction of certain files
    C. transferring of records from one type of file to another
    D. creation of inactive files

25. Assume that, as a supervisor, you are responsible for orienting and training new employees in your unit.
    Which of the following can MOST properly be omitted from your discussions with a new employee?
    A. The purpose of commonly used office forms
    B. Time and leave regulations
    C. Procedures for required handling of routine business calls
    D. The reason the last employee was fired

KEY (CORRECT ANSWERS)

1.	A	11.	A
2.	D	12.	B
3.	B	13.	D
4.	B	14.	D
5.	A	15.	C
6.	C	16.	D
7.	C	17.	C
8.	C	18.	B
9.	B	19.	C
10.	C	20.	D

21.	C
22.	B
23.	A
24.	A
25.	D

EXAMINATION SECTION
TEST 1

DIRECTIONS: Each question or incomplete statement is followed by several suggested answers or completions. Select the one that BEST answers the question or completes the statement. *PRINT THE LETTER OF THE CORRECT ANSWER IN THE SPACE AT THE RIGHT.*

1. The ∧ or caret symbol is a proofreader's mark which means that a
   A. space should have been left between two words
   B. new paragraph should be indicated
   C. word, phrase, or punctuation mark should be inserted
   D. word that is abbreviated should be spelled out

   1.____

2. Of the following items, the one which should NOT be omitted from a typed inter-office memorandum is the
   A. salutation
   B. complementary closing
   C. formal signature
   D. names of those to receive copies

   2.____

3. A typed rough draft should be double-spaced and should have wide margins PRIMARILY in order to
   A. save time in making typing corrections
   B. provide room for making insertions and corrections
   C. insure that the report is well-organized
   D. permit faster typing of the draft

   3.____

4. In tabular reports, when a main heading, secondary heading, and single line of columnar headings are used, a triple space (2 blank lines) would be used after the _____ heading(s).
   A. main
   B. secondary
   C. columnar
   D. main and secondary

   4.____

5. You have been requested to type a letter to Mr. Brown, a district attorney of a small town.
   Of the following, the CORRECT salutation to use is Dear
   A. District Attorney Brown:
   B. Mr. District Attorney:
   C. Mr. Brown:
   D. Honorable Brown:

   5.____

6. A form letter that is sent to the public can be made to look more personal in appearance by doing all of the following EXCEPT
   A. using a meter stamp on the envelope of the letter
   B. having the letter signed with pen and ink
   C. using a good quality of paper for the letter
   D. matching the type used in the letter with that used for fill-ins

   6.____

7. A senior typist opens a word-processing application to instruct a typist to create a table that contains three column headings. Under each column heading are three items.
Of the following, which sequence should the senior typist tell the typist to use when creating this table?
   A. First type the headings, and then type the items under them, a column at a time
   B. type each heading with its column of items under it, one column at a time
   C. first type the column of items, then center the headings above them
   D. type the headings and items across the page line by line

7.____

8. When a letter is addressed to an agency and a particular person should see it, an *attention line* is used.
This attention line is USUALLY found
   A. on the envelope only
   B. above the address
   C. below the address
   D. after the agency named in the address

8.____

9. The typing technique of *justifying* is used to
   A. decide how wide margins of different sized letters should be
   B. make all the lines of copy end evenly on the right-hand margin
   C. center headings above columns on tabular typed material
   D. condense the amount of space that is needed to make a manuscript look presentable

9.____

10. The date line on a letter is typed correctly when the date is ALL on one line
    A. with the month written out   B. with slashes between the numbers
    C. and the month is abbreviated   D. with a period at the end

10.____

11. When considering how wide to make a column when typing a table, the BASIC rule to follow is that the column should be as wide as the longest
    A. item in the body of the column
    B. heading of all of the columns
    C. item in the body or heading of that column
    D. heading or the longest item in the body of any column on that page

11.____

12. When a lengthy quotation is included in a letter or a report, it must be indicated that it is quoted material. This may be done by
    A. enclosing the quotation in parentheses
    B. placing an exclamation point at the end of the quotation
    C. using the apostrophe marks
    D. indenting from the regular margins on the left and right

12.____

13. In order to reach the highest rate of speed and the greatest degree of accuracy while typing, it is LEAST important to
    A. maintain good posture
    B. keep the hands and arms at a comfortable level
    C. strike the keys evenly
    D. keep the typing action in the wrists

14. It has been shown that the rate of typing and dictation drops when the secretary is not familiar with the language or topic of the copy.
    A practice that a supervisor might BEST advise to improve the knowledge and therefore increase the rate of typing dictation for such material would be for the secretary to
    A. plan a conference with her supervisor to discuss the subject matter
    B. read and review correspondence and related technical journals that come into the office
    C. recopy or retype previously transcribed material as practice
    D. withdraw sample materials from the files to take home for study

15. The one of the following in which the tab key is NOT generally used is the
    A. placement of the complimentary close and signature line
    B. indentation of paragraphs
    C. placement of the date line
    D. centering of title headings

16. In order for a business letter to be effective, it is LEAST important that it
    A. say what is meant simply and directly
    B. be written in formal language
    C. include all information the receiver needs to know
    D. be courteously written

17. If you are momentarily called away from your desk while typing a report of a confidential nature, you should cover or turn the copy over and
    A. remove the page being typed from the computer and file the report
    B. ask someone to watch your desk for you
    C. close the document so that the page is not visible
    D. spread a folder over the computer screen to conceal it

18. When typing a table that contains a column of figures and a column of words, the PROPER alignment of the column of figures and the column of words should be an even _____ the column of words.
    A. right-hand edge for the column of numbers and an even left-hand edge for
    B. right-hand edge for both the column of numbers and
    C. left-hand edge for the column of numbers and an even right-hand edge for
    D. left-hand edge for both the column of numbers and

19. The word *re*, when used in a memorandum, refers to the information that is on the _____ line. 19._____
    A. identification   B. subject   C. attention   D. reference

20. Of the following uses of the period, the one which requires NO spacing after it when it is typed is when the period 20._____
    A. follows an abbreviation or an initial
    B. follows a figure or letter at the beginning of a line in a list of items
    C. comes between the initials that make up a single abbreviation
    D. comes at the end of a sentence

21. This <u>mark</u> is a proofreader's mark meaning the word 21._____
    A. is misspelled
    B. should be underlined
    C. should be bold
    D. should be capitalized

22. When typing a report that is double-spaced, the STANDARD recommended practice for indicating the start of new paragraphs is to 22._____
    A. double-space between paragraphs and indent the first word at least five spaces
    B. triple-space between paragraphs and indent the first word at least five spaces
    C. triple-space between paragraphs and type block style at the margin
    D. double-space between paragraphs and type block style at the margin

23. In order to center a heading on a sheet of paper once the center of the paper has been found, the EASIEST and MOST efficient method to use is 23._____
    A. note the scale at each end of the heading to be centered and divide by two
    B. backspace from the center of the paper one space for every two letters and spaces in the heading
    C. arrange the heading around the middle number on the computer
    D. use a ruler to mark off the amount of space from both sides of the center of the paper that should be taken up by the heading

24. You are about to type a single-spaced letter from a typewritten draft. In order to center this letter from top to bottom, your FIRST step should be to 24._____
    A. determine the number of spaces needed for the top and bottom margins
    B. determine the number of spaces needed for the left and right margins
    C. count the number of lines, including blank ones, which will be used for the letter
    D. subtract from the number of writing lines on the sheet of paper the number of lines that will not be used for the letter

25. When typing a table which lists several amounts of money and the total in a column, the dollar sign should be placed in front of the 25._____
    A. first dollar amount only
    B. total dollar amount only
    C. first and total dollar amounts only
    D. all of the amounts of money in the column

26. If a legal document is being prepared and requires necessary information to be typed into blank areas on preprinted legal forms, the margins for a line of typewritten material should be determined PRIMARILY by
    A. counting the total number of words to be typed
    B. the margins set for the pre-printed matter
    C. spacing backwards from the right margin rule
    D. the estimated width and height of the material to be entered

26.____

27. When checking for errors in material you've typed, it is BEST to
    A. proofread the material and use the spell-check function in combination
    B. give the material to someone else to review
    C. run the spell-check function and auto-correct all found errors
    D. proofread the material then e-mail it to another typist for final approval

27.____

28. Assume that Mr. Frank Foran is an acting official. In a letter written to him, the word *acting* would
    A. be used with the title in the address and in the salutation
    B. not be used with the title in the address
    C. be used with the title in the address but not in the salutation
    D. not be used with the title in the address or in the salutation

28.____

29. The software program that requires proficiency in typing in order to best utilize its MOST important features is
    A. Microsoft Excel   B. Adobe Reader
    C. Microsoft Word   D. Intuit QuickBooks

29.____

30. The MAIN reason for keeping a careful record of incoming mail is that
    A. greater speed and accuracy is obtained for answering outgoing mail
    B. this record is legal evidence
    C. it develops the efficiency of the office clerks
    D. the information may be useful some day

30.____

KEY (CORRECT ANSWERS)

1.	C	11.	C	21.	D
2.	D	12.	D	22.	A
3.	B	13.	D	23.	B
4.	B	14.	B	24.	C
5.	C	15.	D	25.	C
6.	A	16.	B	26.	B
7.	D	17.	C	27.	A
8.	C	18.	A	28.	C
9.	B	19.	B	29.	C
10.	A	20.	C	30.	A

TEST 2

DIRECTIONS: Each question or incomplete statement is followed by several suggested answers or completions. Select the one that BEST answers the question or completes the statement. *PRINT THE LETTER OF THE CORRECT ANSWER IN THE SPACE AT THE RIGHT.*

Questions 1-4.

DIRECTIONS: Questions 1 through 4 are to be answered SOLELY on the basis of the information contained in the following passage which is taken from a typing test.

Modern office methods, geared to ever higher speeds and aimed at ever greater efficiency, are largely the result of the typewriter. The typewriter is a substitute for handwriting; and, in the hands of a skilled typist, not only turns out letters and other documents at least three times faster than a penman can do the work, but turns out the greater volume more uniformly and legibly. With the use of carbon paper and onionskin paper, identical copies can be made at the same time.

The typewriter, besides its effect on the conduct of business and government, has had a very important effect on the position of women. The typewriter has done much to bring women into business and government, and today there are vastly more women than men typists. Many women have used the keys of the typewriter to climb the ladder to responsible managerial positions.

The typewriter, as its name implies, employs type to make an ink impression on paper. For many years, the manual typewriter was the standard machine used. Today, the electric typewriter is dominant, with electronic typewriters, word processors, and computers coming into wider use.

The mechanism of the office manual typewriter includes a set of keys arranged systematically in rows; a semicircular frame of type, connected to the keys by levers; the carriage or paper carrier; a rubber roller called a platen, against which the type strikes; and an inked ribbon which makes the impression of the type character when the key strikes it. This machine, once omnipresent, is an antique today.

1. The above passage mentions a number of good features of the combination of a skilled typist and a typewriter.
   Of the following, the feature which is NOT mentioned in the passage is
   A. speed B. uniformity C. reliability D. legibility

   1._____

2. According to the above passage, a skilled typist can
   A. turn out at least five carbon copies of typed matter
   B. type at least three times faster than a penman can write
   C. type more than 80 words a minute
   D. readily move into a managerial position

   2._____

61

3. According to the above passage, which of the following is NOT part of the mechanism of a manual typewriter?
   A. Carbon paper
   B. Paper carrier
   C. Platen
   D. Inked ribbon

   3._____

4. According to the above passage, the typewriter has helped
   A. men more than women in business
   B. women in career advancement into management
   C. men and women equally, but women have taken better advantage of it
   D. more women than men, because men generally dislike routine typing work

   4._____

5. Standard rules for typing spacing have developed through usage. According to these rules, two spaces are left after a(n)
   A. colon
   B. comma
   C. hyphen
   D. opening parenthesis

   5._____

6. Assume that you have to type the heading CENTERING TYPED HEADINGS on a piece of paper which extends from 0 to 100 on the typewriter scale. You want the heading to be perfectly centered on the paper.
   In order to find the proper point on the typewriter scale at which to begin typing, you should determine the paper's center point on the typewriter scale and then _____ the number of letters and spaces in the heading.
   A. add
   B. add one-half
   C. subtract
   D. subtract one-half

   6._____

7. While typing from a rough draft, the practice of reading a line ahead of what you are now typing is considered to be a
   A. *good* practice; it may prepare your fingers for the words which you will be typing
   B. *good* practice; it may help you to review the subject matter contained in the material
   C. *poor* practice; it may increase your typing speed so that your accuracy is decreased
   D. *poor* practice; it may cause you to lose your concentration and make errors in the words you are presently typing

   7._____

8. Assume that you are transcribing a letter and you are not sure how to divide a word at the end of a line you are typing.
   The BEST way to determine where to divide the word is by
   A. asking your supervisor
   B. asking the person who dictated the letter
   C. checking with other stenographers
   D. looking up the word in a dictionary

   8._____

9. When taking proper care of a typewriter, it is NOT a desirable action to
   A. clean the feed rolls with a cloth
   B. dust the exterior surface of the machine
   C. oil the rubber parts of the machine
   D. use a type-cleaning brush to clean the keys

10. Of the following, the LEAST desirable action to take when typing a rough draft of a report is to
    A. cross out typing errors instead of erasing them
    B. double or triple space between lines
    C. provide large margins on all sides of the typing paper
    D. use letterhead or onionskin paper

11. The date line of every business letter should indicate the month, the day of the month, and the year.
    The MOST common practice when typing a date line is to type it as
    A. Jan. 12, 2018
    B. January 12, 2018
    C. 1-12-18
    D. 1/12/18

Questions 12-16.

DIRECTIONS: Questions 12 through 16 are to be answered SOLELY on the basis of the information provided in the following passage.

A written report is a communication of information from one person to another. It is an account of some matter especially investigated, however routine that matter may be. The ultimate basis of any good written report is facts, which became known through observation and verification. Good written reports may seem to be no more than general ideas and opinions. However, in such cases, the facts leading to these opinions were gathered, verified, and reported earlier, and the opinions are dependent upon these facts. Good style, proper form, and emphasis cannot make a good written report out of unreliable information and bad judgments but on the other hand, solid investigation and brilliant thinking are not likely to become very useful until they are effectively communicated to others. If a person's work calls for written reports, then his work is often no better than his written reports.

12. Based on the information in the above passage, it can be concluded that opinions expressed in a report should be
    A. based on facts which are gathered and reported
    B. emphasized repeatedly when they result from a special investigation
    C. kept to a minimum
    D. separated from the body of the report

13. In the above passage, the one of the following which is mentioned as a way of establishing facts is
    A. authority
    B. communication
    C. reporting
    D. verification

14. According to the above passage, the characteristic shared by ALL written reports is that they are
    A. accounts of routine matters
    B. transmissions of information
    C. reliable and logical
    D. written in proper form

    14.____

15. Which of the following conclusions can LOGICALLY be drawn from the information given in the above passage?
    A. Brilliant thinking can make up for unreliable information in a report.
    B. One method of judging an individual's work is the quality of the written reports he is required to submit.
    C. Proper form and emphasis can make a good report out of unreliable information.
    D. Good written reports that seem to be no more than general ideas should be rewritten.

    15.____

16. Which of the following suggested titles would be MOST appropriate for this passage?
    A. GATHERING AND ORGANIZING FACTS
    B. TECHNIQUES OF OBSERVATION
    C. NATURE AND PURPOSE OF REPORTS
    D. REPORTS AND OPINIONS: DIFFERENCES AND SIMILARITIES

    16.____

Questions 17-25

DIRECTIONS: Each of Questions 17 through 25 consists of a sentence which may or may not be an example of good English usage. Examine each sentence, considering grammar, punctuation, spelling, capitalization, and awkwardness. Then choose the correct statement about it from the four choices below it. If the English usage in the sentence given is better than any of the changes suggested in Choices B, C, or D, pick choice A. Do NOT pick a choice that will change the meaning of the sentence.

17. We attended a staff conference on Wednesday the new safety and fire rules were discussed.
    A. This is an example of acceptable writing.
    B. The words *safety*, *fire*, and *rules* should begin with capital letters.
    C. There should be a comma after the word *Wednesday*.
    D. There should be a period after the word *Wednesday*, and the word *the* should begin with a capital letter.

    17.____

18. Neither the dictionary or the telephone directory could be found in the office library.
    A. This is an example of acceptable writing.
    B. The word *or* should be changed to *nor*.
    C. The word *library* should be spelled *libery*.
    D. The word *neither* should be changed to *either*.

    18.____

19. The report would have been typed correctly if the typist cold read the draft.   19._____
    A. This is an example of acceptable writing.
    B. The word *would* should be removed.
    C. The word *have* should be inserted after the word *could*.
    D. The word *correctly* should be changed to *correct*.

20. The supervisor brought the reports and forms to an employees desk.   20._____
    A. This is an example of acceptable writing.
    B. The word *brought* should be changed to *took*.
    C. There should be a comma after the word *reports* and a comma after the word *forms*.
    D. The word *employees* should be spelled *employee's*.

21. It's important for all the office personnel to submit their vacation schedules on time.   21._____
    A. This is an example of acceptable writing.
    B. The word *It's* should be spelled *Its*.
    C. The word *their* should be spelled *they're*.
    D. The word *personnel* should be spelled *personal*.

22. The supervisor wants that all staff members report to the office at 9:00 A.M.   22._____
    A. This is an example of acceptable writing.
    B. The word *that* should be removed and the word *to* should be inserted after the word *members*.
    C. There should be a comma after the word *wants* and a comma after the word *office*.
    D. The word *wants* should be changed to *want* and the word *shall* should be inserted after the word *members*.

23. Every morning the clerk opens the office mail and distributes it.   23._____
    A. This is an example of acceptable writing.
    B. The word *opens* should be changed to *open*.
    C. The word *mail* should be changed to *letters*.
    D. The word *it* should be changed to *them*.

24. The secretary typed more fast on an electric typewriter than on a manual typewriter.   24._____
    A. This is an example of acceptable writing.
    B. The words *more fast* should be changed to *faster*.
    C. There should be a comma after the words *electric typewriter*.
    D. The word *than* should be changed to *then*.

25. The new stenographer needed a desk a typewriter, a chair and a blotter.   25._____
    A. This is an example of acceptable writing.
    B. The word *blotter* should be spelled *blodder*.
    C. The word *stenographer* should begin with a capital letter.
    D. There should be a comma after the word *desk*.

KEY (CORRECT ANSWERS)

1.	C	11.	B
2.	B	12	A
3.	A	13.	D
4.	B	14.	B
5.	A	15.	B
6.	D	16.	C
7.	D	17.	D
8.	D	18.	B
9.	C	19.	C
10.	D	20.	D

21. A
22. B
23. A
24. B
25. D

EXAMINATION SECTION
TEST 1

DIRECTIONS: Each question or incomplete statement is followed by several suggested answers or completions. Select the one that BEST answers the question or completes the statement. *PRINT THE LETTER OF THE CORRECT ANSWER IN THE SPACE AT THE RIGHT.*

Questions 1-25

Each sentence in questions 1-25 includes four words with letters over them. One of these words has been typed incorrectly. Indicate the misspelled word by printing the letter in the space at the right.

1. If the administrator attempts to withold information,
     A   B
there is a good likelihood that there will be serious
          C
repercussions.
   D

2. He condescended to apologize, but we felt that a beligerent
   A   B   C
person should not occupy an influential position.
     D

3. Despite the sporadic delinquent payments of his indebted-
     A   B   C
ness, Mr. Johnson has been an exemplery customer.
   D

4. He was appreciative of the support he consistantly
   A   B
  C   D
acquired, but he felt that he had waited an inordinate
length of time for it.

5. Undeniably they benefited from the establishment of a
  A   B
  C   D
receivership, but the question or statutary limitations
remained unresolved.

1.____

2.____

3.____

4.____

5.____

6.
         A
Mr. Smith profered his hand as an indication that he
      B   C
considered it a viable contract, but Mr. Nelson alluded
        D
to the fact that his colleagues had not been consulted.

7.
           A   B
The treatments were beneficial according to the optomo-
   C   D
trists, and the consensus was that minimal improvement
could be expected.

8.
   A
Her frivalous manner was unbecoming because the air of
   B   C   D
solemnity at the cemetery was pervasive.

9.
     A
The clandestine meetings were designed to make the two
 B   C
adversaries more amicible, but they served only to
    D
intensify their emnity.

10.
           A
Do you think that his innovative ideas and financial
 B   C   D
acumen will help stabalize the fluctuations of the stock
market?

11.
         A
In order to keep a perpetual inventory, you will have to
  B   C   D
keep an uninterrupted surveillance of all the miscellaneous
stock.

12.
        A
She used the art of pursuasion on the children because
   B   C D
she found that caustic remarks had no perceptible effect
on their behavior.

13.
        A   B
His sacreligious outbursts offended his constituents, and
      C   D
he was summarily removed from office by the City Council.

13.____

14.
        A   B
They exhorted the contestants to greater efforts, but the
    C
exhorbitant costs in terms of energy expended resulted in
               D
a feeling of lethargy.

14.____

15.
                   A   B
Since he was knowledgable about illicit drugs, he was
        C   D
served with a subpoena to appear for the prosecution.

15.____

16.
         A   B
In spite of his lucid statements, they denigrated his
                             C D
report and decided it should be succintly paraphrased.

16.____

17.
                      A   B
The discussion was not germane to the contraversy, but
    C   D
the indicted man's insistence on further talk was allowed.

17.____

18.
      A   B
The legislators were enervated by the distances they had
  C   D
traveled during the election year to fulfil their speaking engagements.

18.____

19.
    A   B   C
The plaintiffs' attornies charged the defendant in the
   D
case with felonious assault.

19.____

20.
         A   B
It is symptomatic of the times that we try to placate
                                                          C
all, but a proposal for new forms of disciplinery action
                      D
was promulgated by the staff.

21.
        A
A worrysome situation has developed as a result of the
        B   C
assessment that absenteeism is increasing despite our
       D
conscientious efforts.

22.
         A   B
I concurred with the credit manager that it was practi-
                            C
cable to charge purchases on a biennial basis, and the
                         D
company agreed to adhear to this policy.

23.
                 A   B   C
The pastor was chagrined and embarassed by the irreverent
                     D
conduct of one of his parishioners.

24.
       A   B   C
His inate seriousness was belied by his flippant
D
demeanor.

25.
         A   B   C
It was exceedingly regrettable that the excessive number
    D
of challanges in the court delayed the start of the
trial.

Questions 26-45.

In each of the following sentences, numbered 26-45, there may be an error. Indicate the appropriate correction by printing the corresponding letter in the space at the right. If the sentence is correct as is, indicate this by printing the corresponding letter in the space at the right. Unnecessary changes will be considered incorrect.

26. In that building there seemed to be representatives of Teachers College, the Veterans Bureau, and the Businessmen's Association.   26.____

    A. Teacher's College B. Veteran's Bureau
    C. Businessmens Association D. correct as is

27. In his travels, he visited St. Paul, San Francisco, Springfield, Ohio, and Washington, D.C..   27.____

    A. Ohio and B. Saint Paul
    C. Washington, D.C. D. correct as is

28. As a result of their purchasing a controlling interest in the syndicate, it was well-known that the Bureau of Labor Statistics' calculations would be unimportant.   28.____

    A. of them purchasing B. well known
    C. Statistics D. correct as is

29. Walter Scott, Jr.'s, attempt to emulate his father's success was doomed to failure.   29.____

    A. Junior's, B. Scott's, Jr.,
    C. Scott, Jr.'s attempt D. correct as is

30. About B.C. 250 the Romans invaded Great Britain, and remains of their highly developed civilization can still be seen.   30.____

    A. 250 B.C. B. Britain and
    C. highly-developed D. correct as is

31. The two boss's sons visited the children's department.   31.____

    A. bosses B. bosses'
    C. childrens' D. correct as is

32. Miss Amex not only approved the report, but also decided that it needed no revision.   32.____

    A. report; but B. report but
    C. report. But D. correct as is

33. Here's brain food in a jiffy--economical too!   33.____

    A. economical too! B. 'brain food'
    C. jiffy-economical D. correct as is

34. She said, "He likes the "Gatsby Look" very much."   34.____

    A. said "He B. "he
    C. 'Gatsby Look' D. correct as is

35. We anticipate that we will be able to visit them briefly in Los Angeles on Wednesday after a 5-day visit.

    A. Wednes-
    B. 5-day
    C. briefly
    D. correct as is

36. She passed all her tests, and, she now has a good position.

    A. tests, and she
    B. past
    C. tests;
    D. correct as is

37. The billing clerk said, "I will send the bill today"; however, that was a week ago, and it hasn't arrived yet!

    A. today;"
    B. today,"
    C. ago and
    D. correct as is

38. "She types at more-than-average speed," Miss Smith said, "but I feel that it is a result of marvelous concentration and self control on her part."

    A. more than average
    B. "But
    C. self-control
    D. correct as is

39. The state of Alaska, the largest state in the union, is also the northernmost state.

    A. Union
    B. Northernmost State
    C. State of Alaska
    D. correct as is

40. The memoirs of Ex-President Nixon, will sell more copies than Six Crises, the book he wrote in the 60's.

    A. Six Crises
    B. ex-President
    C. 60s
    D. correct as is

41. He spoke on his favorite topic, "Why We Will Win." (How could I stop him?)

    A. Win".
    B. him?).
    C. him)?
    D. correct as is

42. "All any insurance policy is, is a contract for services," said my insurance agent, Mr. Newton.

    A. Insurance Policy
    B. Insurance Agent
    C. policy is is a
    D. correct as is

43. Inasmuch as the price list has not been up dated, we should send it to the printer.

    A. In as much
    B. updated
    C. pricelist
    D. correct as is

44. We feel that "Our know-how" is responsible for the improvement in technical developments.

    A. "our
    B. know how
    C. that,
    D. correct as is

45. Did Cortez conquer the Incas? the Aztecs? the South American Indians?

    A. Incas, the Aztecs, the South American Indians?
    B. Incas; the Aztecs; the South American Indians?
    C. south American Indians?
    D. correct as is

Questions 46-70.

In the article which follows, certain words or groups of words are underlined and numbered. The underlined word or group of words may be incorrect because they present an error in grammer, usage, sentence structure, capitalization, diction, or punctuation. For each numbered word or group of words, there is an identically numbered question consisting of four choices based only on the underlined portion. For each question numbered 46-70, indicate the best choice by printing the corresponding letter in the space at the right. <u>Unnecessary changes will be considered incorrect</u>.

TIGERS VIE FOR CITY CHAMPIONSHIP

In their second year of varsity football, the North Side Tigers have gained a shot at the city championship. Last Saturday in the play-offs, the Tigers defeated the Western High School Cowboys,<u> thus eliminated that team</u> from contention. Most of the
         46
credit for the team's improvement must go to Joe Harris, the
         47
coach. <u>To play as well as they do</u> now, the coach must have given the team superior instruction. There is no doubt that, <u>if a
         48
coach is effective, his influence is over</u> many young minds.

With this major victory behind them, the Tigers can now look
         49
forward <u>to meet</u> the defending champions, the Revere Minutemen, in the finals.
         50

The win over the Cowboys was <u>due to</u> North Side's supremacy in the air. The Tigers' players have the advantage of strength
         51
and of <u>being speedy</u>. Our sterling quarterback, Butch Carter, a
         52
master of the long pass, used <u>these kind of passes</u> to bedevil the
         53
boys from Western. As a matter of fact, if the Tigers <u>would have used</u> the passing offense earlier in the game, the score would have been more one sided. Butch, by the way, our all-around senior student, has already been tapped for bigger things. Having the
         54
highest marks in his class, <u>Barton College has offered him a scholarship</u>.

The team's defense is another story. During the last few
         55
weeks, neither the linebackers nor the safety man <u>have shown</u> sufficient ability to contain their opponents' running game. In
         56
the city final, <u>the defensive unit's failing to complete it's assignments</u> may lead to disaster. However, the coach said that
         57
this unit <u>not only has been cooperative, but also the coach</u> praised their eagerness to learn. He also said that this team
         58

has not and never will give up. This kind of spirit is contag-
       59
ious, therefore I predict that the Tigers will win because I have
       60
affection and full confidence in the team.
   One of the happy surprises this season is Peter Yisko, our
                    61
punter. Peter is in the United States for only two years. When
he was in grammar school in the old country, it was not necessary
                   62
for him to have studied hard. Now, he depends on the football
                                                          63
team to help him with his English. Everybody but the team mascot
and I have been pressed into service. Peter was ineligible last
                     64
year when he learned that he would only obtain half of the credits
he had completed in Europe. Nevertheless, he attended occasional
practice sessions, but he soon found out that, if one wants to be
                                    65
a successful player, you must realize that regular practice is
required. In fact, if a team is to be successful, it is necessary
                         66
that everyone be present for all practice sessions. "The life of
              67
a football player," says Peter, "is better than a scholar."
                                                68
Facing the Minutemen, the Tigers will meet their most
formidable opposition yet. This team is not only gaining a bad
reputation but also indulging in illegal practices on the field.
                     69
They can't hardly object to us being technical about penalties
under these circumstances. As far as the Minutemen are concerned,
                                     70
a victory will taste sweet like a victory should.

46.   A. , that eliminated that team
      B. and they were eliminated
      C. and eliminated them
      D. correct as is

47.   A. To make them play as well as they do
      B. Having played so well
      C. After they played so well
      D. correct as is

48.   A. if coaches are effective; they have influence over
      B. to be effective, a coach influences
      C. if a coach is effective, he influences
      D. correct as is

49.
- A. to meet with
- B. to meeting
- C. to a meeting of
- D. correct as is

50.
- A. because of
- B. on account of
- C. motivated by
- D. correct as is

51.
- A. operating swiftly
- B. speed
- C. running speedily
- D. correct as is

52.
- A. these kinds of pass
- B. this kind of passes
- C. this kind of pass
- D. correct as is

53.
- A. would be used
- B. had used
- C. were using
- D. correct as is

54.
- A. he was offered a scholarship by Barton College.
- B. Barton College offered a scholarship to him.
- C. a scholarship was offered him by Barton College.
- D. correct as is

55.
- A. had shown
- B. were showing
- C. has shown
- D. correct as is

56.
- A. the defensive unit failing to complete its assignment
- B. the defensive unit's failing to complete its assignment
- C. the defensive unit failing to complete it's assignment
- D. correct as is

57.
- A. has been not only cooperative, but also eager to learn
- B. has not only been cooperative, but also shows eagerness to learn
- C. has been not only cooperative, but also they were eager to learn
- D. correct as is

58.
- A. has not given up and never will
- B. has not and never would give up
- C. has not given up and never will give up
- D. correct as is

59.
- A. .Therefore
- B. : therefore
- C. --therefore
- D. correct as is

60. A. full confidence and affection for
    B. affection for and full confidence in
    C. affection and full confidence concerning
    D. correct as is

61.
    A. is living   B. was living
    C. has been   D. correct as is

62.
    A. to study   B. to be studying
    C. to have been studying   D. correct as is

63. A. but the team mascot and me has
    B. but the team mascot and myself has
    C. but the team mascot and me have
    D. correct as is

64. A. only learned that he would obtain hall
    B. learned that he would obtain only half
    C. learned that he only would obtain half
    D. correct as is

65.
    A. a person   B. everyone
    C. one   D. correct as is

66.
    A. is   B. will be
    C. shall be   D. correct as is

67.
    A. to be a scholar   B. being a scholar
    C. that of a scholar   D. correct as is

68. A. not only is gaining a bad reputation
    B. is gaining not only a bad reputation
    C. is not gaining only a bad reputation
    D. correct as is

69. A. can hardly object to us being
    B. can hardly object to our being
    C. can't hardly object to our being
    D. correct as is

70. A. victory will taste sweet like it should.
    B. victory will taste sweetly as it should taste.
    C. victory will taste sweet as a victory should.
    D. correct as is

KEY (CORRECT ANSWERS

1. B	16. C	31. B	46. C	61. C
2. C	17. B	32. B	47. A	62. A
3. D	18. D	33. D	48. C	63. A
4. B	19. B	34. C	49. B	64. B
5. D	20. C	35. B	50. A	65. C
6. A	21. A	36. A	51. B	66. D
7. B	22. D	37. D	52. C	67. C
8. A	23. B	38. D	53. B	68. D
9. C	24. A	39. A	54. D	69. A
10. C	25. D	40. B	55. C	70. C
11. D	26. D	41. D	56. B	
12. A	27. C	42. D	57. A	
13. A	28. B	43. B	58. B	
14. C	29. D	44. A	59. A	
15. A	30. A	45. D	60. B	

EXAMINATION SECTION
TEST 1

DIRECTIONS: Each question or incomplete statement is followed by several suggested answers or completions. Select the one that BEST answers the question or completes the statement. *PRINT THE LETTER OF THE CORRECT ANSWER IN THE SPACE AT THE RIGHT.*

Questions 1-50.

DIRECTIONS: One word in each of Questions 1 through 50 is MISSPELLED. Indicate the letter of the MISSPELLED word in the space at the right.

1. A. statute   B. stationary   1.____
   C. staturesque   D. stature

2. A. practicible   B. practical   2.____
   C. particle   D. reticule

3. A. plague   B. plaque   C. ague   D. aigrete   3.____

4. A. theology   B. idealogy   4.____
   C. psychology   D. philology

5. A. dilema   B. stamina   5.____
   C. feminine   C. strychnine

6. A. deceit   B. benefit   C. grieve   D. hienous   6.____

7. A. commensurable   B. measurable   7.____
   C. duteable   C. salable

8. A. homogeneous   B. heterogeneous   8.____
   C. advantageous   D. religeous

9. A. criticize   B. dramatise   C. exorcise   D. exercise   9.____

10. A. maintain   B. maintainance   10.____
    C. sustain   D. sustenance

11. A. portend   B. portentious   11.____
    C. pretend   D. pretentious

12. A. prophesize   B. prophesies   12.____
    C. farinaceous   D. spaceous

13. A. choose   B. chose   C. choosen   D. chasten   13.____

14. A. censure   B. censorious   14.____
    C. pleasure   D. pleasurible

15. A. cover   B. coverage   C. adder   D. adege   15.____

16. A. balloon   B. diregible   C. direct   D. descent   16.____

17. A. whemsy   B. crazy   C. flimsy   D. lazy   17._____
18. A. derision   B. pretention   18._____
    C. sustention   D. contention
19. A. question   B. questionaire   19._____
    A. legion   B. legionary
20. A. chattle   B. cattle   C. dismantle   D. kindle   20._____
21. A. canal   B. cannel   C. chanel   D. colonel   21._____
22. A. hemorrage   B. storage   C. manage   D. foliage   22._____
23. A. surgeon   B. sturgeon   C. luncheon   D. stancheon   23._____
24. A. facial   B. physical   C. fiscle   D. muscle   24._____
25. A. congradulate   B. percolate   25._____
    C. major   D. leisure
26. A. convenience   B. privilige   26._____
    C. emerge   D. immerse
27. A. erasable   B. inflammable   27._____
    C. audable   D. laudable
28. A. final   B. fines   C. finis   D. Finish   28._____
29. A. emitted   B. representative   29._____
    C. discipline   D. insistance
30. A. diphthong   B. rarified   C. library   D. recommend   30._____
31. A. compel   B. belligerent   31._____
    C. successful   D. sargeant
32. A. dispatch   B. dispise   C. dispose   D. dispute   32._____
33. A. administrator   B. adviser   33._____
    C. diner   D. celluler
34. A. ignite   B. ignision   C. igneous   D. ignited   34._____
35. A. pallor   B. ballid   C. ballet   D. pallid   35._____
36. A. urbane   B. surburbane   36._____
    C. interurban   D. urban
37. A. symtom   B. serum   37._____
    C. antiseptic   D. aromatic
38. A. register   B. registrar   C. purser   D. burser   38._____
39. A. athletic   B. tragedy   39._____
    C. batallion   D. sophomore

80

40.	A.	latent	B.	godess	C.	aisle	D.	whose	40.____
41.	A.	rhyme	B.	rhythm	C.	thime	D.	thine	41.____
42.	A.	eighth			B.	exaggerate			42.____
	C.	electoral			D.	villain			
43.	A.	statute			B.	superintendent			43.____
	C.	iresistible			D.	colleague			
44.	A.	sieze	B.	therefor	C.	auxiliary	D.	changeable	44.____
45.	A.	siege			B.	knowledge			45.____
	C.	lieutenent			D.	weird			
46.	A.	acquitted			B.	polititian			46.____
	C.	professor			D.	conqueror			
47.	A.	changeable			B.	chargeable			47.____
	C.	salable			D.	useable			
48.	A.	promissory			B.	prisoner			48.____
	C.	excellent			D.	tyrrany			
49.	A.	comptroller			B.	traveled			49.____
	C.	accede			D.	procede			
50.	A.	Britain			B.	Brittainica			50.____
	C.	conductor			D.	vendor			

KEY (CORRECT ANSWERS)

1.	C	11.	B	21.	C	31.	D	41.	C
2.	A	12.	D	22.	A	32.	B	42.	C
3.	D	13.	C	23.	D	33.	D	43.	C
4.	B	14.	D	24.	C	34.	B	44.	A
5.	A	15.	D	25.	A	35.	B	45.	C
6.	D	16.	B	26.	B	36.	B	46.	B
7.	C	17.	A	27.	C	37.	A	47.	D
8.	D	18.	B	28.	D	38.	D	48.	D
9.	B	19.	B	29.	D	39.	C	49.	D
10.	B	20.	A	30.	B	40.	B	50.	B

4 (#1)

CORRECT SPELLING

1. statuesque
2. practicable
3. aigrette
4. ideology
5. dilemma
6. heinous
7. dutiable
8. religious
9. dramatize
10. maintenance
11. portentous
12. spacious
13. chosen
14. pleasurable
15. adage
16. dirigible
17. whimsey or whimsy
18. pretension
19. questionnaire
20. chattel
21. channel
22. hemorrhage
23. stanchion
24. fiscal
25. congratulate
26. privilege
27. audible
28. Finnish
29. insistence
30. rarefied
31. sergeant
32. despise
33. cellular
34. ignition
35. ballad
36. suburban
37. symptom
38. bursar
39. battalion
40. goddess
41. thyme
42. electoral
43. irresistible
44. seize
45. lieutenant
46. politician
47. usable
48. tyranny
49. proceed
50. Britannica

TEST 2

Questions 1-50.

DIRECTIONS: Select the letter of the word or expression that MOST NEARLY expresses the meaning of the capitalized word in the group.

1. FICTITIOUS
   A. turbulent   B. anxious   C. assumed   D. scanty

2. ARDENT
   A. fervid   B. gay   C. savage   D. untamed

3. BLATANT
   A. insipid   B. open   C. closed   D. clamorous

4. DISTRAIT
   A. crooked   B. narrow
   C. broken   D. absentminded

5. EQUITABLE
   A. unbiased   B. unjust
   C. unreasonable   D. unfair

6. EXPEDITE
   A. hinder   B. harm   C. send   D. hasten

7. LUCRATIVE
   A. painful   B. creditable
   C. preferential   D. profitable

8. POSTDATED
   A. past date   B. future date
   C. no date   D. current date

9. RESOURCES
   A. debts   B. liabilities
   C. funds   D. losses

10. AGENDA
    A. receipt   B. agent
    C. combination   D. memoranda

11. DISCRETE
    A. careful   B. prudent   C. truthful   D. separate

12. DOGMATIC
    A. bovine   B. canine   C. opinionated   D. unprincipled

83

13. INTREPID
    A. fearful   B. fearless   C. fanciful   D. cowardly

14. TENACITY
    A. firmness   B. sagacity   C. temerity   D. thinness

15. ASEPTIC
    A. antique   B. artistic   C. sterile   D. austere

16. CREDIBLE
    A. believable   B. unbelievable
    C. correct   D. suitable

17. LESSEE
    A. lender   B. giver   C. receiver   D. renter

18. IGNOMINY
    A. illiteracy   B. ill luck
    C. disgrace   D. despair

19. PRODIGAL
    A. wasteful   B. marvelous   C. ominous   D. harmless

20. VOLUBLE
    A. bulky   B. glib   C. desirable   D. malleable

21. JAMB
    A. doorway   B. crowd   C. fruit   D. animal

22. ATOMIC
    A. combustible   B. minute
    C. crystalline   D. ambient

23. ACUMEN
    A. beauty   B. poise
    C. keen discernment D. illness

24. SUPERCILIOUS
    A. foolish   B. needless   C. callous   D. haughty

25. SPURIOUS
    A. large   B. small
    C. valid   D. not genuine

26. PREDATORY   26.____
    A. plundering   B. fawning
    C. encouraging   D. preceding

27. AMPERSAND   27.____
    A. ammunition   B. currency
    C. abbreviation   D. illumination

28. DEHYDRATED   28.____
    A. airless   B. worthless
    C. waterless   D. pointless

29. NOCTURNAL   29.____
    A. nightly   B. revolving   C. daily   D. frequently

30. DILATORY   30.____
    A. expanding B. delaying   C. watery   D. pickling

31. SANGUINE   31.____
    A. baleful   B. thirsty   C. hopeful   D. delinquent

32. PHLEGMATIC   32.____
    A. sluggish   B. active   C. potent   D. secretive

33. PODIATRIST   33.____
    A. head   B. infants   C. feet   D. adults

34. INGENUE   34.____
    A. fashion   B. state   C. medicine   D. stage

35. CORPOREAL   35.____
    A. military   B. naval   C. bodily   D. legal

36. MUNDANE   36.____
    A. stupid   B. ladylike   C. worldly   D. weedy

37. INTERVENE   37.____
    A. induce   B. insert   C. interfere D. solve

38. IMMINENT   38.____
    A. of high renown   B. impending
    C. very large   D. incurable

39. GERMANE   39.____
    A. Teutonic   B. relevant
    C. infectious   D. brutal

40. PARITY

    A. doubt
    B. equality
    C. fitness
    D. littleness

41. RATIONALIZE

    A. rattle
    B. explain by reason
    C. limit consumption
    D. charge

42. SUCCINCT

    A. superfluous
    B. concise
    C. ponderous
    D. succulent

43. VENIAL

    A. pardonable
    B. revengeful
    C. fearful
    D. despicable

44. VERBOSITY

    A. bitterness
    B. action
    C. wordiness
    D. speed

45. WITHER

    A. canaries
    B. cracks
    C. decay
    D. trills

46. CIRCUMVENT

    A. outwit
    B. surround
    C. open up
    D. cover

47. COMPLICITY

    A. deceit
    B. delight in society
    C. partnership in wrong
    D. relief from debt

48. IPSO FACTO

    A. by that very fact
    B. made by hand
    C. according to him
    D. as a matter of fact

49. ABSTRUSE

    A. profound
    B. absurd
    C. enormous
    D. ridiculous

50. RESTIVE

    A. permanent
    B. quiet
    C. sullen
    D. impatient

KEY (CORRECT ANSWERS)

1. C	11. D	21. A	31. C	41. B
2. A	12. C	22. B	32. A	42. B
3. D	13. B	23. C	33. C	43. A
4. D	14. A	24. D	34. D	44. C
5. A	15. C	25. D	35. C	45. C
6. D	16. A	26. A	36. C	46. A
7. D	17. D	27. C	37. C	47. C
8. B	18. C	28. C	38. B	48. A
9. C	19. A	29. A	39. B	49. A
10. D	20. B	30. B	40. B	50. D

TEST 3

Questions 1-10.

DIRECTIONS: For each word listed below, one correct syllabication is shown. Indicate the CORRECT choice.

1. A. rep er cus sion B. re per cus sion 1.____
   C. rep er cuss ion D. re perc us sion

2. A. corr es pon dence B. cor resp on dence 2.____
   C. cor re spond ence D. cor res pond ence

3. A. sup er in ten dent B. su per in ten dent 3.____
   C. su per int end ent D. su per in tend ent

4. A. ac com mo date B. acc om mod ate 4.____
   C. acc omm o date D. ac com mod ate

5. A. ac know ledge B. ac knowl edge 5.____
   C. ack nowl edge D. ack now ledge

6. A. aud it or ium B. au dit or ium 6.____
   C. aud i tor i um D. au di to ri um

7. A. hosp i tal ize B. hos pit a lize 7.____
   C. hosp it al ize D. hos pi tal ize

8. A. du pli ca tion B. dup lic a tion 8.____
   C. du plic a tion D. dup li ca tion

9. A. re cap i tu late B. rec ap it u late 9.____
   C. re ca pi tu late D. re ca pit u late

10. A. com plim en ta ry B. com pli men ta ry 10.____
    C. comp lim ent ar y D. comp li ment a ry

Questions 11-25.

DIRECTIONS: In each of the following groups of sentences, there are three sentences which are correct and one which is incorrect because it contains an error in usage. Indicate the letter of the INCORRECT sentence.

11. A. There was, in the first place, no indication that a crime had been committed. 11.____
    B. She is taller than any other member of her class.
    C. She decided to leave the book lay on the table.
    D. Haven't you any film in stock at this time?

12. A. Because they had been trained for emergencies, the assault did not catch them by surprise. 12.____
    B. They divided the loot between the four of them in proportion to their effort.
    C. The number of strikes is gradually diminishing.
    D. Between acts we went out to the lobby for a brief chat.

13. A. It is difficult to recollect what life was like before the war. 13._____
    B. Will each of the pupils please hand their home work in?
    C. There are fewer serious mistakes in this pamphlet than I had thought.
    D. "Leave Her to Heaven" is the title of a novel by Ben Ames Williams.

14. A. I was too greatly relieved to be able to say anything. 14._____
    B. These insignia date back to ancient Roman times.
    C. We observed a strange phenomenon; the house seemed to sway in the wind and to tremble like a leaf.
    D. It would be much more preferable if you were no longer seen in his company.

15. A Please send me this data at your earliest convenience. 15._____
    A. The loss of their material proved a severe handicap.
    B. My principal objection to this plan is that it is impracticable.
    C. The doll has lain in the rain all evening.

16. A. I had expected to see my brother. 16._____
    B. He expected to have seen his brother.
    C. I hoped to see you do better.
    D. It was his duty to assist our friend.

17. A. The reason why I am writing to you is that I wish to avoid further misunderstanding. 17._____
    B. These kind of arguments always cause hard feelings.
    C. Regardless of your decision, I shall have to go.
    D. I have only twenty pupils in this class.

18. A. Which is the youngest of the two sisters? 18._____
    B. I am determined to finish the work before Saturday.
    C. It is difficult to see why the problems are not correctly solved.
    D. I have never met a more interesting person.

19. A. Located on a mountainside with a babbling brook beside the door, it was a dream palace. 19._____
    B. Blessed are they that have not seen and yet have believed.
    C. The customs in that part of the country are much different than I expected.
    D. Politics, even in towns of small population, has always attracted ambitious young lawyers.

20. A. Of all my friends he is the one on whom I can most surely depend. 20._____
    B. We value the Constitution because of it's guarantees to freedom.
    C. The audience was deeply stirred by the actor's performance .
    D. Give the book to whoever comes into the room first.

21. A. Everything was in order: the paper ruled, the pencils sharpened, the chairs placed. 21._____
    B. Neither John nor Peter were able to attend the reception.
    C. In April the streets which had been damaged by cold weather were repaired by the workmen.
    D. You may lend my book to the pupil who you think will enjoy it most.

22. A. He fidgeted, like most children do, while the grown-ups were discussing the problem.
    B. I won't go unless you go with me.
    C. Sitting beside the charred ruins of his cabin, the frontiersman told us the story of the attack.
    D. Certainly there can be no objection to the boys" working on a volunteer basis.

23. A. The congregation was dismissed.
    B. The congregation were deeply moved by the sermon.
    C. What kind of an automobile is that?
    D. His explanation and mine agree.

24. A. There is no danger of him being elected.
    B. There is no doubt of his election.
    C. John and he are to be the speakers.
    D. John and she are to be the speakers.

25. A. Them that honor me I will honor.
    B. They that believe in me shall be rewarded.
    C. Who did you see at the meeting?
    D. Whom are you writing to?

KEY (CORRECT ANSWERS)

1.	B	11.	C
2.	C	12.	B
3.	D	13.	B
4.	A	14.	D
5.	B	15.	A
6.	D	16.	B
7.	D	17.	B
8.	A	18.	A
9.	D	19.	C
10.	B	20.	B

21. B
22. A
23. C
24. A
25. C

EXAMINATION SECTION

TEST 1

DIRECTIONS: Each question or incomplete statement is followed by several suggested answers or completions. Select the one that BEST answers the question or completes the statement. *PRINT THE LETTER OF THE CORRECT ANSWER IN THE SPACE AT THE RIGHT.*

1. Which of the following sentences is punctuated INCORRECTLY?
   A. Johnson said, "One tiny virus, Blanche, can multiply so fast that it will become 200 viruses in 25 minutes."
   B. With economic pressures hitting them from all sides, American farmers have become the weak link in the food chain.
   C. The degree to which this is true, of course, depends on the personalities of the people involved, the subject matter, and the atmosphere in general.
   D. "What loneliness, asked George Eliot, is more lonely than distrust?"

1.____

2. Which of the following sentences is punctuated INCORRECTLY?
   A. Based on past experiences, do you expect the plumber to show up late, not have the right parts, and overcharge you.
   B. When polled, however, the participants were most concerned that it be convenient.
   C. No one mentioned the flavor of the coffee, and no one seemed to care that china was used instead of plastic.
   D. As we said before, sometimes people view others as things; they don't see them as living, breathing beings like themselves.

2.____

3. Convention members travelled here from Kingston New York Pittsfield Massachusetts Bennington Vermont and Hartford Connecticut.
   How many commas should there be in the above sentence?
   A. 3   B. 4   C. 5   D. 6

3.____

4. Of the two speakers the one who spoke about human rights is more famous and more humble.
   How many commas should there be in the above sentence?
   A. 1   B. 2   C. 3   D. 4

4.____

5. Which sentence is punctuated INCORRECTLY?
   A. Five people voted no; two voted yes; one person abstained.
   B. Well, consider what has been said here today, but we won't make any promises.
   C. Anthropologists divide history into three major periods: the Stone Age, the Bronze Age, and the Iron Age.
   D. Therefore, we may create a stereotype about people who are unsuccessful; we may see them as lazy, unintelligent, or afraid of success.

5.____

6. Which sentence is punctuated INCORRECTLY?
   A. Studies have found that the unpredictability of customer behavior can lead to a great deal of stress, particularly if the behavior is unpleasant or if the employee has little control over it.
   B. If this degree of emotion and variation can occur in spectator sports, imagine the role that perceptions can play when there are real stakes involved.
   C. At other times, however hidden expectations may sabotage or severely damage an encounter without anyone knowing what happened.
   D. There are usually four issues to look for in a conflict: differences in values, goals, methods, and facts.

Questions 7-10.

DIRECTIONS: Questions 7 through 10 test your ability to distinguish between words that sound alike but are spelled differently and have different meanings. In the following groups of sentences, one of the underlined words is used incorrectly.

7. A. By accepting responsibility for their actions, managers promote trust.
   B. Dropping hints or making illusions to things that you would like changed sometimes leads to resentment.
   C. The entire unit loses respect for the manager and resents the reprimand.
   D. Many people are averse to confronting problems directly; they would rather avoid them.

8. A. What does this say about the effect our expectations have on those we supervise?
   B. In an effort to save time between 9 A.M. and 1 P.M., the staff members devised their own interpretation of what was to be done on these forms.
   C. The taskmaster's principal concern is for getting the work done; he or she is not concerned about the need or interests of employees.
   D. The advisor's main objective was increasing Angela's ability to invest her capitol wisely.

9. A. A typical problem is that people have to cope with the internal censer of their feelings.
   B. Sometimes, in their attempt to sound more learned, people speak in ways that are barely comprehensible.
   C. The council will meet next Friday to decide whether Abrams should continue as representative.
   D. His descent from grace was assured by that final word.

10. A. The doctor said that John's leg had to remain stationary or it would not heal properly.
    B. There is a city ordinance against parking too close to fire hydrants.
    C. Meyer's problem is that he is never discrete when talking about office politics.
    D. Mrs. Thatcher probably worked harder than any other British Prime Minister had ever worked.

Questions 11-20.

DIRECTIONS: For each of the following groups of sentences in Questions 11 through 20, select the sentence which is the BEST example of English usage and grammar.

11. A. She is a woman who, at age sixty, is distinctly attractive and cares about how they look.
    B. It was a seemingly impossible search, and no one knew the problems better than she.
    C. On the surface, they are all sweetness and light, but his morbid character is under it.
    D. The minicopier, designed to appeal to those who do business on the run like architects in the field or business travelers, weigh about four pounds.

11.____

12. A. Neither the administrators nor the union representative regret the decision to settle the disagreement.
    B. The plans which are made earlier this year were no longer being considered.
    C. I would have rode with him if I had known he was leaving at five.
    D. I don't know who she said had it.

12.____

13. A. Writing at a desk, the memo was handed to her for immediate attention.
    B. Carla didn't water Carl's plants this week, which she never does.
    C. Not only are they good workers, with excellent writing and speaking skills, and they get to the crux of any problem we hand them.
    D. We've noticed that this enthusiasm for undertaking new projects sometimes interferes with his attention to detail.

13.____

14. A. It's obvious that Nick offends people by being unruly, inattentive, and having no patience.
    B. Marcia told Genie that she would have to leave soon.
    C. Here are the papers you need to complete your investigation.
    D. Julio was startled by you're comment.

14.____

15. A. The new manager has done good since receiving her promotion, but her secretary has helped her a great deal.
    B. One of the personnel managers approached John and tells him that the client arrived unexpectedly.
    C. If somebody can supply us with the correct figures, they should do so immediately.
    D. Like zealots, advocates seek power because they want to influence the policies and actions of an organization.

15.____

16. A. Between you and me, Chris probably won't finish this assignment in time. 16.___
    B. Rounding the corner, the snack bar appeared before us.
    C. Parker's radical reputation made to the Supreme Court his appointment impossible.
    D. By the time we arrived, Marion finishes briefing James and returns to Hank's office.

17. A. As we pointed out earlier, the critical determinant of the success of middle managers is their ability to communicate well with others. 17.___
    B. The lecturer stated there wasn't no reason for bad supervision.
    C. We are well aware whose at fault in this instance.
    D. When planning important changes, it's often wise to seek the participation of others because employees often have much valuable ideas to offer.

18. A. Joan had ought to throw out those old things that were damaged when the roof leaked. 18.___
    B. I spose he'll let us know what he's decided when he finally comes to a decision.
    C. Carmen was walking to work when she suddenly realized that she had left her lunch on the table as she passed the market.
    D. Are these enough plants for your new office?

19. A. First move the lever forward, and then they should lift the ribbon casing before trying to take it out. 19.___
    B. Michael finished quickest than any other person in the office.
    C. There is a special meeting for we committee members today at 4 p.m.
    D. My husband is worried about our having to work overtime next week.

20. A. Another source of conflicts are individuals who possess very poor interpersonal skills. 20.___
    B. It is difficult for us to work with him on projects because these kinds of people are not interested in team building.
    C. Each of the departments was represented at the meeting.
    D. Poor boy, he never should of past that truck on the right.

Questions 21-28.

DIRECTIONS: In Questions 21 through 28, there may be a problem with English grammar or usage. If a problem does exist, select the letter that indicates the most effective change. If no problem exists, select Choice A.

21. He rushed her to the hospital and stayed with her, even though this took quite a bit of his time, he didn't charge her anything. 21.___
    A. No changes are necessary.
    B. Change even though to although
    C. Change the first comma to a period and capitalize even
    D. Change rushed to had rushed

22. Waiting that appears unfairly feels longer than waiting that seems justified. 22.____
    A. No changes are necessary.
    B. Change unfairly to unfair
    C. Change appears to seems
    D. Change longer to longest

23. May be you and the person who argued with you will be able to reach an agreement. 23.____
    A. No changes are necessary
    B. Change will be to were
    C. Change argued with to had an argument with
    D. Change May be to Maybe

24. Any one of them could of taken the file while you were having coffee. 24.____
    A. No changes are necessary
    B. Change any one to anyone
    C. Change of to have
    D. Change were having to were out having

25. While people get jobs or move from poverty level to better paying employment, they stop receiving benefits and start paying taxes. 25.____
    A. No changes are necessary
    B. Change While to As
    C. Change stop to will stop
    D. Change get to obtain

26. Maribeth's phone rang while talking to George about the possibility of their meeting Tom at three this afternoon. 26.____
    A. No changes are necessary
    B. Change their to her
    C. Move to George so that it follows Tom
    D. Change talking to she was talking

27. According to their father, Lisa is smarter than Chris, but Emily is the smartest of the three sisters. 27.____
    A. No changes are necessary
    B. Change their to her
    C. Change is to was
    D. Make two sentences, changing the second comma to a period and omitting but

28. Yesterday, Mark and he claim that Carl took Carol's ideas and used them inappropriately. 28.____
    A. No changes are necessary
    B. Change claim to claimed
    C. Change inappropriately to inappropriate
    D. Change Carol's to Carols'

Questions 29-34.

DIRECTIONS: For each group of sentences in Questions 29 through 34, select the choice that represents the BEST editing of the problem sentence.

29. The managers expected employees to be at their desks at all times, but they would always be late or leave unannounced. 29.____
    A. The managers wanted employees to always be at their desks, but they would always be late or leave unannounced.
    B. Although the managers expected employees to be at their desks no matter what came up, they would always be late and leave without telling anyone.
    C. Although the managers expected employees to be at their desks at all times, the managers would always be late or leave without telling anyone.
    D. The managers expected the employee to never leave their desks, but they would always be late or leave without telling anyone.

30. The one who is department manager he will call you to discuss the problem tomorrow morning at 10 A.M. 30.____
    A. The one who is department manager will call you tomorrow morning at ten to discuss the problem.
    B. The department manager will call you to discuss the problem tomorrow at 10 A.M.
    C. Tomorrow morning at 10 A.M., the department manager will call you to discuss the problem.
    D. Tomorrow morning the department manager will call you to discuss the problem.

31. A conference on child care in the workplace the $200 cost of which to attend may be prohibitive to childcare workers who earn less than that weekly. 31.____
    A. A conference on child care in the workplace that costs $200 may be too expensive for childcare workers who earn less than that each week.
    B. A conference on child care in the workplace, the cost of which to attend is $200, may be prohibitive to childcare workers who earn less than that weekly.
    C. A conference on child care in the workplace who costs $200 may be too expensive for childcare workers who earn less than that a week.
    D. A conference on child care in the workplace which costs $200 may be too expensive to childcare workers who earn less than that on a weekly basis.

32. In accordance with estimates recently made, there are 40,000 to 50,000 nuclear weapons in our world today. 32.____
    A. Because of estimates recently, there are 40,000 to 50,000 nuclear weapons in the world today.
    B. In accordance with estimates made recently, there are 40,000 to 50,000 nuclear weapons in the world today.

C. According to estimates made recently, there are 40,000 to 50,000 weapons in the world today.
D. According to recent estimates, there are 40,000 to 50,000 nuclear weapons in the world today.

33. Motivation is important in problem solving, but they say that excessive motivation can inhibit the creative process.   33._____
    A. Motivation is important in problem solving, but, as they say, too much of it can inhibit the creative process.
    B. Motivation is important in problem solving and excessive motivation will inhibit the creative process.
    C. Motivation is important in problem solving, but excessive motivation can inhibit the creative process.
    D. Motivation is important in problem solving because excessive motivation can inhibit the creative process.

34. In selecting the best option calls for consulting with all the people that are involved in it.   34._____
    A. In selecting the best option consulting with all people concerned with it.
    B. Calling for the best option, we consulted all the affected people.
    C. We called all the people involved to select the best option.
    D. To be sure of selecting the best option, one should consult all the people involved.

35. There are a number of problems with the following letter. From the options below, select the version that is MOST in accordance with standard business style, tone, and form.   35._____

    Dear Sir:

    We are so sorry that we have had to backorder your order for 15,000 widgets and 2,300 whatzits for such a long time. We have been having incredibly bad luck lately. When your order first came in no one could get to it because my secretary was out with the flu and her replacement didn't know what she was doing, then there was the dock strike in Cucamonga which held things up for awhile, and then it just somehow got lost. We think it may have fallen behind the radiator.
    We are happy to say that all these problems have been taken care of, we are caught up on supplies, and we should have the stuff to you soon, in the near future—about two weeks. You may not believe us after everything you've been through with us, but it's true.
    We'll let you know as soon as we have a secure date for delivery. Thank you so much for continuing to do business with us after all the problems this probably has caused you.

    Yours very sincerely,
    Rob Barker

A. Dear Sir:

We are so sorry that we have had to backorder your order for 15,000 widgets and 2,300 whatzits. We have been having problems with staff lately and the dock strike hasn't helped anything.

We are happy to say that all these problems have been taken care of. I've told my secretary to get right on it, and we should have the stuff to you soon. Thank you so much for continuing to do business with us after all the problems this must have caused you.

We'll let you know as soon as we have a secure date for delivery.

Sincerely,
Rob Barker

B. Dear Sir:

We regret that we haven't been able to fill your order for 15,000 widgets and 2,300 whatzits in a timely fashion.

We'll let you know as soon as we have a secure date for delivery.

Sincerely,
Rob Barker

C. Dear Sir:

We are so very sorry that we haven't been able to fill your order for 15,000 widgets and 2,300 whatzits. We have been having incredibly bad luck lately, but things are much better now.

Thank you so much for bearing with us through all of this. We'll let you know as soon as we have a secure date for delivery.

Sincerely,
Rob Barker

D. Dear Sir:

We are very sorry that we haven't been able to fill your order for 15,000 widgets and 2,300 whatzits. Due to unforeseen difficulties, we have had to back-order your request. At this time, supplies have caught up to demand, and we foresee a delivery date within the next two weeks.

We'll let you know as soon as we have a secure date for delivery. Thank you for your patience.

Sincerely,
Rob Barker

KEY (CORRECT ANSWERS)

1.	D	11.	B	21.	C	31.	A
2.	A	12.	D	22.	B	32.	D
3.	B	13.	D	23.	D	33.	C
4.	A	14.	C	24.	C	34.	D
5.	B	15.	D	25.	B	35.	D
6.	C	16.	A	26.	D		
7.	B	17.	A	27.	A		
8.	D	18.	D	28.	B		
9.	A	19.	D	29.	C		
10.	C	20.	C	30.	B		

TESTS IN SPELLING

EXAMINATION SECTION
TEST 1

DIRECTIONS: In each question of the following tests, select the letter of the one MIS-SPELLED word in each of the listed groups of five (5) words. *PRINT THE LETTER OF THE CORRECT ANSWER IN THE SPACE AT THE RIGHT.*

#	A.	B.	C.	D.	E.	Ans.
1.	break	scenary	business	arouse	religious	1.____
2.	rinsed	height	jewel	furtile	doesn't	2.____
3.	perform	divide	apologize	occasion	acheive	3.____
4.	asending	benefit	disappear	operate	grammar	4.____
5.	forty	precede	annuel	parable	curiosity	5.____
6.	irritable	stupefy	gaseous	millionair	luscious	6.____
7.	invincible	Slav	supersede	haddock	fatigueing	7.____
8.	scissors	explanatory	bituminus	heifer	cessation	8.____
9.	caramel	Wisconsin	acquarium	sterilize	pseudonym	9.____
10.	precipise	knapsack	brilliance	challenge	decrepit	10.____
11.	certificate	ajourn	apparel	aggression	symphony	11.____
12.	Norwegian	constent	interruption	wouldn't	article	12.____
13.	heros	logical	guarantee	imprison	legitimate	13.____
14.	happiness	weird	miscellaneous	village	arguement	14.____
15.	wretched	tendency	controversiel	arbitrary	denial	15.____
16.	lonliness	safeguard	pilot	chiefs	obstacle	16.____
17.	shining	professional	scheme	excitment	expectancy	17.____
18.	negative	editorial	clothe	economize	suprising	18.____
19.	illegal	opinion	discription	rationalize	picnicking	19.____
20.	circuit	sponser	exasperate	volume	valuable	20.____

KEY (CORRECT ANSWERS)

1. B. scenery
2. D. fertile
3. E. achieve
4. A. ascending
5. C. annual
6. D. millionaire
7. E. fatiguing
8. C. bituminous
9. C. aquarium
10. A. precipice
11. B. adjourn
12. B. constant
13. A. heroes
14. E. argument
15. C. controversial
16. A. loneliness
17. D. excitement
18. E. surprising
19. C. description
20. B. sponsor

TEST 2

DIRECTIONS: In each question of the following tests, select the letter of the one MISSPELLED word in each of the listed groups of five (5) words. *PRINT THE LETTER OF THE CORRECT ANSWER IN THE SPACE AT THE RIGHT.*

1. A. procession   B. performance   C. poize   D. allied   E. discipline   1._____
2. A. advocate   B. saleries   C. commercial   D. expense   E. forcibly   2._____
3. A. enormous   B. enterprise   C. florist   D. humilliate   E. careful   3._____
4. A. treachery   B. bolstor   C. simplify   D. revelation   E. reciprocal   4._____
5. A. witness   B. derisive   C. typewriter   D. relative   E. medecine   5._____
6. A. betrayel   B. forsaken   C. impetuous   D. finesse   E. recognize   6._____
7. A. forcast   B. pastime   C. several   D. ridiculous   E. cleanliness   7._____
8. A. correspond   B. conceited   C. implies   D. receptacle   E. amatuer   8._____
9. A. captain   B. definitely   C. credited   D. cordially   E. couragous   9._____
10. A. parallel   B. various   C. obnoxious   D. assurence   E. grateful   10._____
11. A. feirce   B. ascent   C. allies   D. doctor   E. coming   11._____
12. A. hopeless   B. absense   C. foretell   D. certain   E. similar   12._____
13. A. advise   B. muscle   C. manual   D. provocation   E. copywright   13._____
14. A. behooves   B. reservoir   C. frostbiten   D. squalor   E. ambuscade   14._____
15. A. systematic   B. precious   C. tremenduous   D. insulation   E. brilliant   15._____
16. A. significant   B. jurisdiction   C. libel   D. monkies   E. legacy   16._____
17. A. delicatessen   B. occupansy   C. gorgeous   D. consolation   E. anxiety   17._____
18. A. tyranny   B. perennial   C. catagory   D. inspector   E. confidential   18._____
19. A. symbol   B. formerly   C. warring   D. caution   E. bankrupcy   19._____
20. A. aperture   B. cellaphane   C. diagnosis   D. intestinal   E. mahogany   20._____

KEY (CORRECT ANSWERS)

1. C. poise
2. B. salaries
3. D. humiliate
4. B. bolster
5. E. medicine
6. A. betrayal
7. A. forecast
8. E. amateur
9. E. courageous
10. D. assurance
11. A. fierce
12. B. abscence
13. E. copyright
14. C. frostbitten
15. C. tremendous
16. D. monkeys
17. B. occupancy
18. C. category
19. E. bankruptcy
20. B. cellophane

TEST 3

DIRECTIONS: In each question of the following tests, select the letter of the one MIS-SPELLED word in each of the listed groups of five (5) words. *PRINT THE LETTER OF THE CORRECT ANSWER IN THE SPACE AT THE RIGHT.*

1. A. pitiful B. latter C. ommitted D. agreement E. reconcile 1.____
2. A. banaana B. routine C. likewise D. indecent E. habitually 2.____
3. A. relieve B. copys C. ninety D. crowded E. electoral 3.____
4. A. adviseable B. illustrative C. financial D. nevertheless E. chimneys 4.____
5. A. prisioner B. immediate C. statistics D. surgeon E. treachery 5.____
6. A. option B. extradite C. comparitive D. jealousy E. illusion 6.____
7. A. handicaped B. assurance C. sympathy D. speech E. dining 7.____
8. A. recommend B. carraige C. disapprove D. independent E. mortgage 8.____
9. A. systematic B. ingenuity C. tenet D. uncanny E. intrigueing 9.____
10. A. arduous B. hideous C. fervant D. companies E. breach 10.____
11. A. together B. attempt C. loyality D. innocent E. rinse 11.____
12. A. argueing B. emergency C. kindergarten D. religious E. schedule 12.____
13. A. society B. anticipate C. dissatisfy D. responsable E. temporary 13.____
14. A. chaufeur B. grammar C. planned D. dining room E. accurate 14.____
15. A. confidence B. maturity C. aspiration D. evasion E. insurence 15.____
16. A. unnecessary B. dirigible C. transparant D. similar E. appetite 16.____
17. A. regional B. slimy C. tumbler D. educator E. femenine 17.____
18. A. orchestration B. proclamation C. pretext D. rearmement E. invoice 18.____
19. A. fragrant B. independent C. halves D. parallel E. advantagous 19.____
20. A. championing B. conversion C. predominent D. puppet E. anarchist 20.____

KEY (CORRECT ANSWERS)

1. C. omitted
2. A. banana
3. B. copies
4. A. advisable
5. A. prisoner
6. C. comparative
7. A. handicapped
8. B. carriage
9. E. intriguing
10. C. fervent
11. C. loyalty
12. A. arguing
13. D. responsible
14. A. chauffeur
15. E. insurance
16. C. transparent
17. E. feminine
18. D. rearmament
19. E. advantageous
20. C. predominant

TEST 4

DIRECTIONS: In each question of the following tests, select the letter of the one MIS-SPELLED word in each of the listed groups of five (5) words. *PRINT THE LETTER OF THE CORRECT ANSWER IN THE SPACE AT THE RIGHT.*

1. A. wrist B. welfare C. necessity D. scenery E. tendancy 1.____
2. A. commiting B. accusation C. endurance D. agreeable E. excitable 2.____
3. A. despair B. surgury C. privilege D. appreciation E. journeying 3.____
4. A. cameos B. propaganda C. delicious D. heathen E. interupt 4.____
5. A. relieve B. disappear C. development D. matress E. ninety-nine 5.____
6. A. finally B. bulitin C. doctor D. desirable E. sincerely 6.____
7. A. wrest B. array C. auspices D. sacrafice E. generations 7.____
8. A. liquid B. vegetable C. silence D. familiar E. fasinate 8.____
9. A. tomato B. suspence C. leisure D. license E. permanent 9.____
10. A. characteristic B. soliciting C. repititious D. immediately E. extravagant 10.____
11. A. travel B. conductor C. equiping D. proposal E. twofold 11.____
12. A. philosopher B. minority C. managment D. emergency E. bibliography 12.____
13. A. constructive B. employee C. stalwart D. masterpeice E. theoretical 13.____
14. A. dissappoint B. volcanic C. illiterate D. myth E. superficial 14.____
15. A. totally B. penninsula C. sandwich D. ripening E. salvation 15.____
16. A. pastel B. aisle C. primarly D. journalistic E. diminished 16.____
17. A. warrier B. unification C. enamel D. defendant E. sustained 17.____
18. A. incidental B. lubricent C. conversion D. jurisdiction E. interpretation 18.____
19. A. auxilary B. boundaries C. session D. fabric E. ceiling 19.____
20. A. imperious B. depreciate C. rebutal D. wharf E. giddy 20.____

KEY (CORRECT ANSWERS)

1. E. tendency
2. A. committing
3. B. surgery
4. E. interrupt
5. D. mattress
6. B. bulletin
7. D. sacrifice
8. E. fascinate
9. B. suspense
10. C. repetitious
11. C. equipping
12. C. management
13. D. masterpiece
14. A. disappoint
15. B. peninsula
16. C. primarily
17. A. warrior
18. B. lubricant
19. A. auxiliary
20. C. rebuttal

TEST 5

DIRECTIONS: In each question of the following tests, select the letter of the one MISSPELLED word in each of the listed groups of five (5) words. *PRINT THE LETTER OF THE CORRECT ANSWER IN THE SPACE AT THE RIGHT.*

1. A. renewel   B. charitable   C. abrupt   D. humankind   E. strengthen   1._____
2. A. khaki   B. survival   C. laboratory   D. intensefied   E. stature   2._____
3. A. diesel   B. cocoa   C. alphabettical   D. visible   E. overlaid   3._____
4. A. neutral   B. ballot   C. parallysis   D. enterprise   E. abnormal   4._____
5. A. ironical   B. mountainous   C. permissible   D. carburetor   E. blizard   5._____
6. A. penalty   B. affidavit   C. document   D. notery   E. valid   6._____
7. A. provocative   B. apparition   C. forfiet   D. procedure   E. requisite   7._____
8. A. terrifying   B. museum   C. minimum   D. competitors   E. efficiensy   8._____
9. A. hangar   B. spokesman   C. mustache   D. cathederal   E. pumpkin   9._____
10. A. guidance   B. until   C. usage   D. loyalist   E. prarie   10._____
11. A. obnoxious   B. balancing   C. squadron   D. illicit   E. clearence   11._____
12. A. timetable   B. gymnasium   C. humid   D. disolve   E. gracious   12._____
13. A. spiciness   B. biblography   C. injunction   D. mediator   E. discriminate   13._____
14. A. endearing   B. mannerism   C. predecesser   D. gardener   E. instantaneous   14._____
15. A. shrewdness   B. purified   C. acceptable   D. uniqueness   E. corugated   15._____
16. A. baptize   B. diversity   C. parochial   D. abandonning   E. hypnosis   16._____
17. A. deteryorate   B. priority   C. cuddle   D. shrivel   E. narcotic   17._____
18. A. neutrality   B. horseradish   C. contemporaries   D. inducement   E. prelimnery   18._____
19. A. eventually   B. disilusioned   C. divine   D. inimitable   E. fraudulent   19._____
20. A. verticle   B. musician   C. tomatoes   D. athletic   E. decision   20._____

KEY (CORRECT ANSWERS)

1. A. renewal
2. D. intensified
3. C. alphabetical
4. C. paralysis
5. E. blizzard
6. D. notary
7. C. forfeit
8. E. efficiency
9. D. cathedral
10. E. prairie
11. E. clearance
12. D. dissolve
13. B. bibliography
14. C. predecessor
15. E. corrugated
16. D. abandoning
17. A. deteriorate
18. E. preliminary
19. B. disillusioned
20. A. vertical

TEST 6

DIRECTIONS: In each question of the following tests, select the letter of the one MISSPELLED word in each of the listed groups of five (5) words. *PRINT THE LETTER OF THE CORRECT ANSWER IN THE SPACE AT THE RIGHT.*

1. A. advising   B. recognize   C. seize   D. supply   E. tradegy   1._____
2. A. intensive   B. stationary   C. benifit   D. equipped   E. preferring   2._____
3. A. predjudice   B. pervade   C. excel   D. capitol   E. chimneys   3._____
4. A. all right   B. ninty   C. cronies   D. nervous   E. separate   4._____
5. A. atheletic   B. queue   C. furl   D. schedule   E. abusing   5._____
6. A. skein   B. wholesome   C. witches   D. coherent   E. defenite   6._____
7. A. aggravate   B. counsel   C. deplorable   D. proficency   E. catarrh   7._____
8. A. suppressed   B. lugubrious   C. pecuniary   D. boulevard   E. fourty-fourth   8._____
9. A. militarism   B. pilot   C. crimnal   D. monotonous   E. tendency   9._____
10. A. prevalent   B. berth   C. auxiliary   D. priveleges   E. women's   10._____
11. A. incurred   B. cieling   C. strengthen   D. carnage   E. typical   11._____
12. A. twins   B. year's   C. acutely   D. changible   E. facility   12._____
13. A. deliscious   B. enormous   C. likeness   D. witnesses   E. commodity   13._____
14. A. scenes   B. enlargement   C. discretion   D. acknowledging   E. sesion   14._____
15. A. annum   B. strenuous   C. tretchery   D. infamy   E. opportune   15._____
16. A. marmelade   B. loot   C. kinsman   D. crochet   E. hawser   16._____
17. A. fireman   B. glossary   C. tuition   D. dissapoint   E. refrigerator   17._____
18. A. inadequate   B. municpal   C. bored   D. masonic   E. utilize   18._____
19. A. partisan   B. temporary   C. cawleflower   D. obstinacy   E. hyperbole   19._____
20. A. people's   B. spherical   C. foliage   D. everlasting   E. feesable   20._____

KEY (CORRECT ANSWERS)

1. E. tragedy
2. C. benefit
3. A. prejudice
4. B. ninety
5. A. athletic
6. E. definite
7. D. proficiency
8. E. forty-fourth
9. C. criminal
10. D. privileges
11. B. ceiling
12. D. changeable
13. A. delicious
14. E. session
15. C. treachery
16. A. marmalade
17. D. disappoint
18. B. municipal
19. C. cauliflower
20. E. feasible

TEST 7

DIRECTIONS: In each question of the following tests, select the letter of the one MIS-SPELLED word in each of the listed groups of five (5) words. *PRINT THE LETTER OF THE CORRECT ANSWER IN THE SPACE AT THE RIGHT.*

#	A	B	C	D	E	Ans
1.	inferred	whisle	jovial	conscript	gracious	1.____
2.	tantalizing	ominous	conductor	duchess	telagram	2.____
3.	reconcile	primitive	sausy	quinine	cede	3.____
4.	immagine	viaduct	chisel	Saturn	currant	4.____
5.	amplify	greace	cholera	perilous	theology	5.____
6.	pursevere	deodorize	ligament	illuminate	dropsy	6.____
7.	legible	frivolously	precious	rezemblence	congeal	7.____
8.	intramural	epidemic	germicide	anonymous	acurracy	8.____
9.	affable	hazard	combustable	lacquer	stationary	9.____
10.	sagacious	interpreter	poultise	dinosaur	dismal	10.____
11.	acknowledging	deligate	foliage	staid	loot	11.____
12.	gardian	losing	notwithstanding	worlds	typhoid	12.____
13.	medal	utilize	efficiency	apricot	soliceting	13.____
14.	museum	Christian	possesion	occasional	bored	14.____
15.	capitol	sieze	premises	fragrance	tonnage	15.____
16.	requisition	faculties	canon	chaufur	stomach	16.____
17.	solemn	ascertain	I'll	chef	delinquant	17.____
18.	parliments	distributor	voluntary	lovable	counsel	18.____
19.	morale	democrat	rhumatism	dormitory	leased	19.____
20.	screech	missapropriating	courtesies	wretched	furlough	20.____

KEY (CORRECT ANSWERS)

1. B. whistle
2. E. telegram
3. C. saucy
4. A. imagine
5. B. grease
6. A. persevere
7. D. resemblance
8. E. accuracy
9. C. combustible
10. C. poultice
11. B. delegate
12. A. guardian
13. E. soliciting
14. C. possession
15. B. seize
16. D. chauffeur
17. E. delinquent
18. A. parliaments
19. C. rheumatism
20. B. misappropriating

TEST 8

DIRECTIONS: In each question of the following tests, select the letter of the one MISSPELLED word in each of the listed groups of five (5) words. *PRINT THE LETTER OF THE CORRECT ANSWER IN THE SPACE AT THE RIGHT.*

#	A	B	C	D	E	Ans
1.	typhoid	tarriff	visible	accent	countries	1.___
2.	dizzy	leggings	steak	compaine	interior	2.___
3.	profit	tiranny	shocked	response	innocent	3.___
4.	freshman	vague	larsiny	ignorant	worrying	4.___
5.	disatesfied	jealous	unfortunately	economical	lettuce	5.___
6.	based	primarily	condemned	accompanied	dupped	6.___
7.	superntendant	veil	congenial	quantities	ere	7.___
8.	unanimous	dessert	undoubtedly	kolera	nuisance	8.___
9.	woman's	bulletin	'tis	Pullman	envellop	9.___
10.	initiate	guardian	pagent	wretched	adieu	10.___
11.	continually	guild	vegtable	vague	patience	11.___
12.	desease	parole	gallery	awkward	you'd	12.___
13.	border	warrant	operated	economics	ilegal	13.___
14.	fatal	agatation	obliged	studying	resignation	14.___
15.	ammendment	promptness	glimpse	canon	tract	15.___
16.	wholly	apricot	destruction	pappal	leisure	16.___
17.	issuing	rabbid	unauthorized	parasite	khaki	17.___
18.	nowadays	courtesies	negotiate	gaurdian	derrick	18.___
19.	partisan	seanse	vacancy	fragrance	corps	19.___
20.	equipped	nuisance	phrenoligist	foreign	insignia	20.___

KEY (CORRECT ANSWERS)

1. B. tariff
2. D. company
3. B. tyranny
4. C. larceny
5. A. dissatisfied
6. E. duped
7. A. superintendent
8. D. cholera
9. E. envelope
10. C. pageant
11. C. vegetable
12. A. disease
13. E. illegal
14. B. agitation
15. A. amendment
16. D. papal
17. B. rabid
18. D. guardian
19. B. seance
20. C. phrenologist

TEST 9

DIRECTIONS: In each question of the following tests, select the letter of the one MISSPELLED word in each of the listed groups of five (5) words. *PRINT THE LETTER OF THE CORRECT ANSWER IN THE SPACE AT THE RIGHT.*

1.	A.	frightfully	B.	mantain	C.	post office	D.	specific	E.	bachelor	1.____
2.	A.	cease	B.	turkeys	C.	woman's	D.	hustling	E.	weild	2.____
3.	A.	expedition	B.	valuoble	C.	typhoid	D.	grapevines	E.	advice	3.____
4.	A.	echoes	B.	absolutly	C.	foggy	D.	wretched	E.	Sabbath	4.____
5.	A.	screech	B.	motorist	C.	congresionel	D.	utilize	E.	eligible	5.____
6.	A.	quizzes	B.	coarse	C.	aquaintence	D.	exhibition	E.	totally	6.____
7.	A.	principle	B.	transferring	C.	statutes	D.	here's	E.	sergeon	7.____
8.	A.	porcilane	B.	primeval	C.	suite	D.	unauthorized	E.	declension	8.____
9.	A.	commodity	B.	mischevious	C.	galvanized	D.	ordinance	E.	tuition	9.____
10.	A.	Christian	B.	fraternity	C.	accompanying	D.	disernable	E.	inadequate	10.____
11.	A.	subsidy	B.	inference	C.	chronicle	D.	purchace	E.	adroit	11.____
12.	A.	resources	B.	cargoes	C.	oponent	D.	disbelief	E.	treasurer	12.____
13.	A.	origional	B.	provincial	C.	knuckle	D.	ridiculous	E.	ecstasy	13.____
14.	A.	attitude	B.	soloes	C.	occurred	D.	policies	E.	technique	14.____
15.	A.	opinionated	B.	quantity	C.	systematic	D.	drought	E.	confidencial	15.____
16.	A.	interim	B.	idleness	C.	accesion	D.	elite	E.	fungi	16.____
17.	A.	inarticulate	B.	servitude	C.	ejaculate	D.	herewith	E.	preceedence	17.____
18.	A.	experimental	B.	minority	C.	cultural	D.	expedient	E.	penant	18.____
19.	A.	apparently	B.	criticism	C.	justification	D.	physican	E.	simultaneous	19.____
20.	A.	accidentally	B.	overule	C.	unintentional	D.	talented	E.	maturation	20.____

KEY (CORRECT ANSWERS)

1. B. maintain
2. E. wield
3. B. valuable
4. B. absolutely
5. C. congressional
6. C. acquaintance
7. E. surgeon
8. A. porcelain
9. B. mischievous
10. D. discernible
11. D. purchase
12. C. opponent
13. A. original
14. B. solos
15. E. confidential
16. C. accession
17. E. precedence
18. E. pennant
19. D. physician
20. B. overrule

TEST 10

DIRECTIONS: In each question of the following tests, select the letter of the one MISSPELLED word in each of the listed groups of five (5) words. PRINT THE LETTER OF THE CORRECT ANSWER IN THE SPACE AT THE RIGHT.

1. A. liabillity B. capacity C. guidance D. illegible E. expedient 1._____
2. A. debris B. apetite C. mosquitoes D. vessal E. yacht 2._____
3. A. tireless B. feindish C. recruit D. swarthy E. sandal 3._____
4. A. redouble B. wizard C. murderer D. hindrance E. syncope 4._____
5. A. equalize B. turbulent C. repetitive D. corronation E. statistical 5._____
6. A. remittance B. sensitivity C. fatality D. soprano E. inconveniance 6._____
7. A. fraternity B. plebeian C. inteligible D. trickster E. expeditionary 7._____
8. A. gasous B. consistency C. brooches D. magistrate E. translucent 8._____
9. A. lightning B. persistent C. cynical D. musician E. recipricate 9._____
10. A. commodity B. fictitous C. rabid D. gaiety E. couldn't 10._____
11. A. visible B. creditor C. paradice D. infinite E. questionnaire 11._____
12. A. existence B. disarming C. endorsement D. commercal E. trigger 12._____
13. A. aluminum B. stuning C. allowance D. irate E. pleasantry 13._____
14. A. cipher B. colloquial C. envoy D. pursued E. writting 14._____
15. A. insurable B. benign C. influential D. sophomore E. casualty 15._____
16. A. presentiment B. theological C. anatamy D. eccentricity E. amphibious 16._____
17. A. embargo B. vocalize C. recommend D. confering E. remunerate 17._____
18. A. tangent B. fickel C. circuit D. mathematics E. vegetarian 18._____
19. A. unscheduled B. declension C. secretariat D. forsight E. enamel 19._____
20. A. hygienic B. arrogant C. disbanded D. census E. memorandem 20._____

KEY (CORRECT ANSWERS)

1. A. liability
2. B. appetite
3. B. fiendish
4. C. murderer
5. D. coronation
6. E. inconvenience
7. C. intelligible
8. A. gaseous
9. E. reciprocate
10. B. fictitious
11. C. paradise
12. D. commercial
13. B. stunning
14. E. writing
15. C. influential
16. C. anatomy
17. D. conferring
18. B. fickle
19. D. foresight
20. E. memorandum

TESTS IN SPELLING

EXAMINATION SECTION
TEST 1

DIRECTIONS: In each question of the following tests, select the letter of the one MIS-SPELLED word in each of the listed groups of five (5) words. *PRINT THE LETTER OF THE CORRECT ANSWER IN THE SPACE AT THE RIGHT.*

#	A.	B.	C.	D.	E.	Answer
1.	barely	assigned	mechanical	concequently	lovingly	1.____
2.	obedient	elaborate	disgust	bearing	ambasador	2.____
3.	awkward	charitable	typhoid	compitition	ruffle	3.____
4.	concervatory	ninth	morsel	squirrels	luxury	4.____
5.	loyalty	occasional	hosiery	bungalow	undicided	5.____
6.	efficient	suberb	achievement	bored	specimen	6.____
7.	adaquate	salaries	utilize	alcohol	colonel	7.____
8.	forcibly	guardian	preceeding	quartile	quizzes	8.____
9.	seiges	unanimous	ridiculous	everlasting	omissions	9.____
10.	itemized	ignoramus	adige	adieu	nickel	10.____
11.	resources	fileal	nervous	logical	certificate	11.____
12.	wiring	turkeys	morass	obvious	bigimmy	12.____
13.	affirmitive	noisy	clothe	carnage	perceive	13.____
14.	ignorant	literally	humerists	business	awkward	14.____
15.	thermometer	tragady	partisan	kinsman	grandiose	15.____
16.	fundamental	herald	delinquent	kindergarden	ascertain	16.____
17.	apropriation	year's	vacancy	enthusiastic	dormitory	17.____
18.	crochet	courtesies	troup	occasionally	spirits	18.____
19.	typewriting	inadequate	legitimate	fuelless	restarant	19.____
20.	tabloux	cooperage	wrapped	tenant	referring	20.____

KEY (CORRECT ANSWERS)

1. D. consequently
2. E. ambassador
3. D. competition
4. A. conservatory
5. E. undecided
6. B. suburb
7. A. adequate
8. C. preceding OR proceeding
9. A. sieges
10. C. adage
11. B. filial
12. E. bigamy
13. A. affirmative
14. C. humorists
15. B. tragedy
16. D. kindergarten
17. A. appropriation
18. C. troop OR troupe
19. E. restaurant
20. A. tableaux OR tableaus

TEST 2

DIRECTIONS: In each question of the following tests, select the letter of the one MIS-SPELLED word in each of the listed groups of five (5) words. *PRINT THE LETTER OF THE CORRECT ANSWER IN THE SPACE AT THE RIGHT.*

1. A. loot B. surgery C. breif D. talcum E. Christmas 1._____
2. A. commenced B. congenial C. fatal D. politician E. standerd 2._____
3. A. unbarable B. physician C. potato D. wiring E. adorable 3._____
4. A. error B. regretted C. instetute D. typhoid E. we're 4._____
5. A. merly B. opportunity C. patterns D. unctious E. righteous 5._____
6. A. luxury B. forty C. control D. originally E. intemate 6._____
7. A. plague B. ignorance C. poltrey D. hence E. bruise 7._____
8. A. athletic B. exebition C. leased D. interrupt E. spirits 8._____
9. A. destruction B. prairie C. quartet D. status E. competators 9._____
10. A. triumph B. utility C. loyalty D. antisapte E. crochet 10._____
11. A. lieutenant B. recrute C. thermometer D. quantities E. usefulness 11._____
12. A. wholly B. sitting C. probably D. criticism E. lynche 12._____
13. A. anteque B. galvanized C. mercantile D. academy E. defense 13._____
14. A. kinsman B. declaration C. absurd D. dispach E. patience 14._____
15. A. opportune B. abbuting C. warranted D. refrigerator E. raisin 15._____
16. A. deffered B. principalship C. lovable D. athletic E. conveniently 16._____
17. A. mislaid B. receipted C. skedule D. mission E. whereabouts 17._____
18. A. tuition B. unnatural C. remodel D. consequence E. misdameanor 18._____
19. A. assessment B. advises C. embassys D. border E. leased 19._____
20. A. morale B. legitemate C. infamy D. indebtedness E. technical 20._____

KEY (CORRECT ANSWERS)

1. C. brief
2. E. standard
3. A. unbearable
4. C. institute
5. A. merely
6. E. intimate
7. C. poultry OR paltry
8. B. exhibition
9. E. competition
10. D. anticipate
11. B. recruit
12. E. lynch
13. A. antique
14. D. dispatch
15. B. abutting
16. A. deferred OR differed
17. C. schedule
18. E. misdemeanor
19. C. embassies
20. B. legitimate

TEST 3

DIRECTIONS: In each question of the following tests, select the letter of the one MISSPELLED word in each of the listed groups of five (5) words. *PRINT THE LETTER OF THE CORRECT ANSWER IN THE SPACE AT THE RIGHT.*

1. A. stepfather B. fireman C. loot D. conclusivly E. commodity 1.____
2. A. mislaid B. roommate C. religous D. thesis E. temporary 2.____
3. A. statutes B. malice C. unbridled D. aisle E. cavelry 3.____
4. A. aknowledge B. immensely C. quantities D. erratic E. postponed 4.____
5. A. people's B. foreign C. obsticles D. opportunity E. cordially 5.____
6. A. fragrance B. burgaleries C. clothe D. twins E. herculean 6.____
7. A. warranted B. yoke C. democrat D. parashute E. Bible 7.____
8. A. existance B. enthusiasm C. medal D. sandwiches E. dunce 8.____
9. A. loyalty B. eternal C. chanceler D. psychology E. assessment 9.____
10. A. bungalow B. mutilate C. forcible D. ridiculous E. cawcus 10.____
11. A. lieutenant B. abandoned C. successor D. phisycal E. inquiries 11.____
12. A. nuisance B. coranation C. voluntary D. faculties E. awe 12.____
13. A. indipendance B. notwithstanding C. tariff D. opportune E. accompanying 13.____
14. A. statutes B. rhubarb C. corset D. prurient E. subsedy 14.____
15. A. partisan B. initiate C. colonel D. ilness E. errant 15.____
16. A. acquired B. wrapped C. propriater D. screech E. dune 16.____
17. A. sufrage B. countenance C. fraternally D. undo E. fireman 17.____
18. A. ladies B. chef C. spirituelist D. Sabbath E. itemized 18.____
19. A. ere B. interests C. cheesecloth D. paridoxical E. garish 19.____
20. A. bulletin B. neutral C. porttiere D. discretion E. inconvenienced 20.____

KEY (CORRECT ANSWERS)

1. D. conclusively
2. C. religious
3. E. cavalry
4. A. acknowledge
5. C. obstacles
6. B. burglaries
7. D. parachute
8. A. existence
9. C. chancellor
10. E. caucus
11. D. physical
12. B. coronation
13. A. independence
14. E. subsidy
15. D. illness
16. C. proprietor
17. A. suffrage
18. C. spiritualist
19. D. paradoxical
20. C. portiere

TEST 4

DIRECTIONS: In each question of the following tests, select the letter of the one MIS-SPELLED word in each of the listed groups of five (5) words. *PRINT THE LETTER OF THE CORRECT ANSWER IN THE SPACE AT THE RIGHT.*

1. A. I'd B. premises C. hysterics D. aparantly E. faculties 1.____
2. A. discipline B. ajurnment C. bachelor D. lose E. wrapped 2.____
3. A. simular B. bulletin C. lovable D. bored E. quizzes 3.____
4. A. attendance B. preparation C. refrigerator D. cafateria E. twelfth 4.____
5. A. inconvenienced B. courtesies C. raisin D. hosiery E. politicean 5.____
6. A. reccommendation B. colonel C. sandwiches D. women's E. undoubtedly 6.____
7. A. technical B. imediately C. temporarily D. dormitory E. voluntary 7.____
8. A. salaries B. abandoned C. consistent D. unconcious E. herald 8.____
9. A. duly B. leer C. emphasise D. vacant E. requisition 9.____
10. A. melancholy B. citrus C. omissions D. bazaar E. derigable 10.____
11. A. acquired B. mercury C. stetistics D. thought E. vassal 11.____
12. A. tempature B. calendar C. series D. gout E. alcohol 12.____
13. A. important B. foreigner C. Australia D. leggend E. rhythm 13.____
14. A. height B. achevement C. monarchial D. axle E. fertile 14.____
15. A. falsity B. prestige C. conquer D. arketecture E. Jerusalem 15.____
16. A. magnifecent B. bacteria C. holly D. diseases E. cellar 16.____
17. A. medicine B. grievous C. beaker D. benefits E. attendents 17.____
18. A. military B. vacancy C. weird D. feudalism E. hybird 18.____
19. A. adopted B. agrigate C. Renaissance D. tournament E. colonies 19.____
20. A. vivisection B. penitentiary C. candadacy D. seer E. Sabbath 20.____

KEY (CORRECT ANSWERS)

1. D. apparently
2. B. adjournment
3. A. similar
4. D. cafeteria
5. E. politician
6. A. recommendation
7. B. immediately
8. D. unconscious
9. C. emphasizes or emphasis
10. E. dirigible
11. C. statistics
12. A. temperature
13. D. legend
14. B. achievement
15. D. architecture
16. A. magnificent
17. E. attendants
18. E. hybrid
19. B. aggregate
20. C. candidacy

TEST 5

DIRECTIONS: In each question of the following tests, select the letter of the one MISSPELLED word in each of the listed groups of five (5) words. *PRINT THE LETTER OF THE CORRECT ANSWER IN THE SPACE AT THE RIGHT.*

1. A. acknowledging B. deligate C. foliage D. staid E. loot 1.____
2. A. gandar B. losing C. notwithstanding D. worlds E. torrent 2.____
3. A. medal B. utilize C. efficiency D. apricot E. soliceting 3.____
4. A. museum B. Christian C. possesion D. occasional E. bored 4.____
5. A. capitol B. sieze C. premises D. fragrance E. tonnage 5.____
6. A. requisition B. faculties C. canon D. chaufur E. stomach 6.____
7. A. solemn B. ascertain C. I'll D. chef E. delinquant 7.____
8. A. parliments B. distributor C. voluntary D. lovable E. counsel 8.____
9. A. morale B. democrat C. rhumatism D. dormitory E. leased 9.____
10. A. screech B. missapropriating C. courtesies D. wraith E. furlough 10.____
11. A. tryst B. tarriff C. visible D. accent E. contraries 11.____
12. A. dizzy B. leggings C. steak D. compaine E. interior 12.____
13. A. profit B. tiranny C. shocked D. response E. innocent 13.____
14. A. freshman B. vague C. larsiny D. ignorant E. worrying 14.____
15. A. disatesfied B. jealous C. unfortunately D. economical E. lettuce 15.____
16. A. based B. primarily C. condemned D. accompanied E. dupped 16.____
17. A. superntendant B. veil C. congenial D. quantities E. ere 17.____
18. A. unanimous B. dessert C. undoubtedly D. kolera E. nuisance 18.____
19. A. woman's B. bolero C. 'tis D. Pullman E. envellop 19.____
20. A. initiate B. grist C. pagent D. mention E. adieu 20.____

KEY (CORRECT ANSWERS)

1. B. delegate
2. A. gander
3. E. soliciting
4. C. possession
5. B. seize
6. D. chauffeur
7. E. delinquent
8. A. parliaments
9. C. rheumatism
10. B. misappropriating
11. B. tariff
12. D. campaign
13. B. tyranny
14. C. larceny
15. A. dissatisfied
16. E. duped
17. A. superintendent
18. D. cholera
19. E. envelope
20. C. pageant

TEST 6

DIRECTIONS: In each question of the following tests, select the letter of the one MISSPELLED word in each of the listed groups of five (5) words. *PRINT THE LETTER OF THE CORRECT ANSWER IN THE SPACE AT THE RIGHT.*

1. A. attach B. voucher C. twins D. assistence E. cordial 1.____
2. A. faculties B. people's C. indetedness D. ignorant E. resource 2.____
3. A. wholly B. apitite C. twelfth D. unauthorized E. embroider 3.____
4. A. certified B. attorneys C. foggy D. potato E. extravigent 4.____
5. A. hysterics B. simelar C. intelligent D. label E. salaries 5.____
6. A. apponants B. we're C. finely D. herald E. continuous 6.____
7. A. cancellation B. athletic C. perminant D. preference E. utilize 7.____
8. A. urns B. zephyr C. tuition D. incidentally E. aquisition 8.____
9. A. kinsaan B. bazaar C. foliage D. wretched E. asassination 9.____
10. A. insignia B. bimonthly C. typewriting D. notariety E. psychology 10.____
11. A. continually B. guild C. vegtable D. vague E. patience 11.____
12. A. desease B. parole C. gallery D. awkward E. you'd 12.____
13. A. border B. warrant C. operated D. economics E. ilegal 13.____
14. A. fatal B. agatation C. obliged D. studying E. resignation 14.____
15. A. ammendment B. promptness C. glimpse D. canon E. tract 15.____
16. A. wholly B. apricot C. destruction D. pappal E. leisure 16.____
17. A. issuing B. rabbid C. unusual D. parasite E. khaki 17.____
18. A. nowadays B. courtesies C. negotiate D. gaurdian E. derrick 18.____
19. A. partisan B. seanse C. vacancy D. fragrance E. corps 19.____
20. A. equipped B. nuisance C. phrenology D. foriegn E. insignia 20.____

KEY (CORRECT ANSWERS)

1. D. assistance
2. C. indebtedness
3. B. appetite
4. E. extravagant
5. B. similar
6. A. opponents
7. C. permanent
8. E. acquisition
9. E. assassination
10. D. notoriety
11. C. vegetable
12. A. disease
13. E. illegal
14. B. agitation
15. A. amendment
16. D. papal
17. B. rabid
18. D. guardian
19. B. eance
20. D. foreign

TEST 7

DIRECTIONS: In each question of the following tests, select the letter of the one MIS-SPELLED word in each of the listed groups of five (5) words. *PRINT THE LETTER OF THE CORRECT ANSWER IN THE SPACE AT THE RIGHT.*

1. A. frightfully B. mantain C. post office D. specific E. bachelor 1._____
2. A. cease B. turkeys C. woman's D. hustling E. weild 2._____
3. A. expidition B. valuing C. typhoid D. grapevines E. advice 3._____
4. A. balance B. visible C. correspondant D. etc. E. arctic 4._____
5. A. benefit B. arkives C. classified D. inasmuch E. sincerity 5._____
6. A. obedient B. vengeance C. plague D. fascinate E. contageous 6._____
7. A. desicion B. partner C. economy D. piece E. arrogant 7._____
8. A. dyeing B. lightning C. millenary D. undulate E. embarrass 8._____
9. A. strenuous B. isicle C. panel D. suburb E. luxury 9._____
10. A. aisle B. proffer C. people's D. condemed E. morale 10._____
11. A. advising B. recognizing C. seize D. supply E. tradegy 11._____
12. A. intensive B. stationary C. benifit D. equipped E. preferring 12._____
13. A. predjudice B. pervade C. excel D. capitol E. chimera 13._____
14. A. all right B. ninty C. cronies D. nervous E. separate 14._____
15. A. atheletic B. queue C. schedule D. furl E. credible 15._____
16. A. inevitable B. sincerly C. monkeys D. definite E. cynical 16._____
17. A. niece B. accommodate C. loveliness D. reciept E. forcibly 17._____
18. A. cancel B. chagrined C. allies D. playwright E. liutenant 18._____
19. A. pageant B. alcohol C. villian D. Odyssey E. criticize 19._____
20. A. acknowledge B. article C. contemptible D. taciturn E. sovreign 20._____

KEY (CORRECT ANSWERS)

1. B. maintain
2. E. wield
3. A. expedition
4. C. correspondent
5. B. archives
6. E. contagious
7. A. decision
8. C. millinery
9. B. icicle
10. D. condemned
11. E. tragedy
12. C. benefit
13. A. prejudice
14. B. ninety
15. A. athletic
16. B. sincerely
17. D. receipt
18. E. lieutenant
19. C. villain
20. E. sovereign

TEST 8

DIRECTIONS: In each question of the following tests, select the letter of the one MIS-SPELLED word in each of the listed groups of five (5) words. *PRINT THE LETTER OF THE CORRECT ANSWER IN THE SPACE AT THE RIGHT.*

1. A. incurred B. cieling C. strengthen D. carnage E. typical 1.____
2. A. twins B. year's C. acutely D. changible E. facility 2.____
3. A. deliscious B. enormous C. likeness D. witnesses E. commodity 3.____
4. A. scenes B. enlargement C. discretion D. acknowledging E. sesion 4.____
5. A. annum B. strenuous C. tretchery D. infamy E. opportune 5.____
6. A. marmelade B. loot C. kinsman D. crochet E. hawser 6.____
7. A. sophmore B. duly C. across D. lovable E. propaganda 7.____
8. A. quantities B. rickety C. roommate D. penetentiary E. lose 8.____
9. A. interrupt B. cauldron C. convienient D. successor E. apiece 9.____
10. A. acquire B. incesent C. forfeit D. typewritten E. dysentery 10.____
11. A. inferred B. whisle C. jovial D. conscript E. gracious 11.____
12. A. tantalizing B. ominous C. conductor D. duchess E. telegram 12.____
13. A. reconcile B. primitive C. sausy D. quinine E. cede 13.____
14. A. immagine B. viaduct C. chisel D. Saturn E. currant 14.____
15. A. amplify B. greace C. cholera D. perilous E. theology 15.____
16. A. pursevere B. deodorize C. ligament D. illuminate E. dropsy 16.____
17. A. cavalier B. transparent C. perjury D. vicinaty E. navigate 17.____
18. A. postpone B. dictaphone C. corral D. alligator E. arteficial 18.____
19. A. cannon B. hospital C. distilliry D. righteous E. secession 19.____
20. A. matrimony B. digestable C. scrutiny D. artisan E. mediocre 20.____

KEY (CORRECT ANSWERS)

1. B. ceiling
2. D. changeable
3. A. delicious
4. E. session
5. C. treachery
6. A. marmalade
7. A. sophomore
8. D. penitentiary
9. C. convenient
10. B. incessant
11. B. whistle
12. E. telegram
13. C. saucy
14. A. imagine
15. B. grease
16. A. persevere
17. D. vicinity
18. E. artificial
19. C. distillery
20. B. digestible

TEST 9

DIRECTIONS: In each question of the following tests, select the letter of the one MISSPELLED word in each of the listed groups of five (5) words. *PRINT THE LETTER OF THE CORRECT ANSWER IN THE SPACE AT THE RIGHT.*

1. A. feirce   B. ascent   C. allies   D. doctor   E. coming   1._____
2. A. hopeless   B. absense   C. foretell   D. certain   E. similar   2._____
3. A. advise   B. muscle   C. manual   D. provocation   E. copywright   3._____
4. A. behooves   B. reservoir   C. frostbiten   D. squalor   E. ambuscade   4._____
5. A. systematic   B. precious   C. tremendos   D. insulation   E. brilliant   5._____
6. A. significant   B. jurisdiction   C. libel   D. monkies   E. legacy   6._____
7. A. dual   B. authentic   C. serenety   D. mechanism   E. suburban   7._____
8. A. candel   B. dissolution   C. laceration   D. portend   E. pigeon   8._____
9. A. loyalty   B. periodic   C. presume   D. led   E. suprano   9._____
10. A. mania   B. medicinal   C. dungarees   D. overwelming   E. masquerade   10._____
11. A. pitiful   B. latter   C. ommitted   D. agreement   E. reconcile   11._____
12. A. bananna   B. routine   C. likewise   D. indecent   E. habitually   12._____
13. A. relieve   B. copys   C. ninety   D. crowded   E. electoral   13._____
14. A. adviseable   B. illustrative   C. financial   D. nevertheless   E. chimneys   14._____
15. A. prisioner   B. immediate   C. statistics   D. surgeon   E. abscond   15._____
16. A. option   B. extradite   C. comparitive   D. jealousy   E. illusion   16._____
17. A. handicaped   B. assurance   C. sympathy   D. speech   E. dining   17._____
18. A. recommend   B. carraige   C. disapprove   D. independent   E. mortgage   18._____
19. A. systematic   B. ingenuity   C. tenet   D. uncanny   E. intrigueing   19._____
20. A. arduous   B. hideous   C. fervant   D. companies   E. breach   20._____

KEY (CORRECT ANSWERS)

1. A. fierce
2. B. absence
3. E. copyright
4. C. frostbitten
5. C. tremendous
6. D. monkeys
7. C. serenity
8. A. candle
9. E. soprano
10. D. overwhelming
11. C. omitted
12. A. banana
13. B. copies
14. A. advisable
15. A. prisoner
16. C. comparative
17. A. handicapped
18. B. carriage
19. E. intriguing
20. C. fervent

TEST 10

DIRECTIONS: In each question of the following tests, select the letter of the one MISSPELLED word in each of the listed groups of five (5) words. *PRINT THE LETTER OF THE CORRECT ANSWER IN THE SPACE AT THE RIGHT.*

1. A. together   B. attempt   C. loyality   D. innocent   E. rinse   1._____
2. A. argueing   B. emergency   C. kindergarten D. religious   E. schedule   2._____
3. A. society   B. anticipate   C. dissatisfy   D. responsable E. temporary   3._____
4. A. chaufeur   B. grammar   C. planned   D. dining room E. accurate   4._____
5. A. confidence B. maturity   C. aspirations D. evasion   E. insurence   5._____
6. A. unnecessary B. dirigible   C. transparant D. similar   E. appetite   6._____
7. A. treachery   B. comedian   C. arrest   D. recollect   E. mistep   7._____
8. A. falsify   B. blight   C. flexible   D. drasticaly E. meddlesome   8._____
9. A. congestion B. publickly   C. receipts   D. academic   E. paralyze   9._____
10. A. possibilities B. undergoes C. consistant   D. aggression E. pledge   10._____
11. A. wrist   B. welfare   C. necessity   D. scenery   E. tendancy   11._____
12. A. commiting B. accusation   C. endurance   D. agreeable   E. excitable   12._____
13. A. despair   B. surgury   C. privilege   D. appreciation E. journeying 13._____
14. A. cameos   B. propaganda   C. delicious   D. heathen   E. interupt   14._____
15. A. relieve   B. disappear   C. development D. matress   E. ninety-nine 15._____
16. A. finally   B. bullitin   C. doctor   D. desirable   E. sincerely   16._____
17. A. wrest   B. array   C. auspices   D. sacrafice   E. generations 17._____
18. A. liquid   B. vegetable   C. silence   D. familiar   E. fasinate   18._____
19. A. tomato   B. suspence   C. leisure   D. license   E. permanent   19._____
20. A. characteristic B. soliciting C. repitious D. immediately E. extravagant 20._____

KEY (CORRECT ANSWERS)

1. C. loyalty
2. A. arguing
3. D. responsible
4. A. chauffeur
5. E. insurance
6. C. transparent
7. E. misstep
8. D. drastically
9. B. publicly
10. C. consistent
11. E. tendency
12. A. committing
13. B. surgery
14. E. interrupt
15. D. mattress
16. B. bulletin
17. D. sacrifice
18. E. fascinate
19. B. suspense
20. C. repetitious

RECORD KEEPING
EXAMINATION SECTION
TEST 1

DIRECTIONS: Each question or incomplete statement is followed by several suggested answers or completions. Select the one that BEST answers the question or completes the statement. *PRINT THE LETTER OF THE CORRECT ANSWER IN THE SPACE AT THE RIGHT.*

Questions 1-15.

DIRECTIONS: Questions 1 through 15 are to be answered on the basis of the following list of company names below. Arrange a file alphabetically, word-by-word, disregarding punctuation, conjunctions, and apostrophes. Then answer the questions.

    A Bee C Reading Materials
    ABCO Parts
    A Better Course for Test Preparation
    AAA Auto Parts Co.
    A-Z Auto Parts, Inc.
    Aabar Books
    Abbey, Joanne
    Boman-Sylvan Law Firm
    BMW Autowerks
    C Q Service Company
    Chappell-Murray, Inc.
    E&E Life Insurance
    Emcrisco
    Gigi Arts
    Gordon, Jon & Associates
    SOS Plumbing
    Schmidt, J.B. Co.

1. Which of these files should appear FIRST?
   A. ABCO Parts
   B. A Bee C Reading Materials
   C. A Better Course for Test Preparation
   D. AAA Auto Parts Co.

2. Which of these files should appear SECOND?
   A. A-Z Auto Parts, Inc.
   B. A Bee C Reading Materials
   C. A Better Course for Test Preparation
   D. AAA Auto Parts Co.

3. Which of these files should appear THIRD?
   A. ABCO Parts
   B. A Bee C Reading Materials
   C. Aabar Books
   D. AAA Auto Parts Co.

4. Which of these files should appear FOURTH?
   A. Aabar Books
   B. ABCO Parts
   C. Abbey, Joanne
   D. AAA Auto Parts Co.

5. Which of these files should appear LAST?
   A. Gordon, Jon & Associates
   B. Gigi Arts
   C. Schmidt, J.B. Co.
   D. SOS Plumbing

6. Which of these files should appear between A-Z Auto Parts, Inc. and Abbey, Joanne?
   A. A Bee C Reading Materials
   B. AAA Auto Parts Co.
   C. ABCO Parts
   D. A Better Course for Test Preparation

7. Which of these files should appear between ABCO Parts and Aabar Books?
   A. A Bee C Reading Materials
   B. Abbey, Joanne
   C. Aabar Books
   D. A-Z Auto Parts

8. Which of these files should appear between Abbey, Joanne and Boman-Sylvan Law Firm?
   A. A Better Course for Test Preparation
   B. BMW Autowerks
   C. Chappell-Murray, Inc.
   D. Aabar Books

9. Which of these files should appear between Abbey, Joanne and C Q Service?
   A. A-Z Auto Parts, Inc.
   B. BMW Autowerks
   C. Choices A and B
   D. Chappell-Murray, Inc.

10. Which of these files should appear between C Q Service Company and Emcrisco?
    A. Chappell-Murray, Inc.
    B. E&E Life Insurance
    C. Gigi Arts
    D. Choices A and B

11. Which of these files should NOT appear between C Q Service Company and E&E Life Insurance?
    A. Gordon, Jon & Associates
    B. Emcrisco
    C. Gigi Arts
    D. All of the above

12. Which of these files should appear between Chappell-Murray, Inc. and   12._____
    Gigi Arts?
    A. C Q Service Inc., E&E Life Insurance, and Emcrisco
    B. Emcrisco, E&E Life Insurance, and Gordon, Jon & Associates
    C. E&E Life Insurance, and Emcrisco
    D. Emcrisco and Gordon, Jon & Associates

13. Which of these files should appear between Gordon, Jon & Associates and   13._____
    SOS Plumbing?
    A. Gigi Arts   B. Schmidt, J.B. Co.
    C. Choices A and B   D. None of the above

14. Each of the choices lists the four files in their proper alphabetical order   14._____
    EXCEPT
    A. E&E Life Insurance; Gigi Arts; Gordon, Jon & Associates; SOS Plumbing
    B. E&E Life Insurance; Emcrisco; Gigi Arts; SOS Plumbing
    C. Emcrisco; Gordon, Jon & Associates; SOS Plumbing; Schmidt, J.B. Co.
    D. Emcrisco; Gigi Arts; Gordon, Jon & Associates; SOS Plumbing

15. Which of the choices lists the four files in their proper alphabetical order?   15._____
    A. Gigi Arts; Gordon, Jon & Associates; SOS Plumbing; Schmidt, J.B. Co.
    B. Gordon, Jon & Associates; Gigi Arts; Schmidt, J.B. Co.; SOS Plumbing
    C. Gordon, Jon & Associates; Gigi Arts; SOS Plumbing; Schmidt, J.B. Co.
    D. Gigi Arts; Gordon, Jon & Associates; Schmidt, J.B. Co.; SOS Plumbing

16. The alphabetical filing order of two businesses with identical names is   16._____
    determined by the
    A. length of time each business has been operating
    B. addresses of the businesses
    C. last name of the company president
    D. no one of the above

17. In an alphabetical filing system, if a business name includes a number, it should   17._____
    be
    A. disregarded
    B. considered a number and placed at the end of an alphabetical section
    C. treated as though it were written in words and alphabetized accordingly
    D. considered a number and placed at the beginning of an alphabetical
       section

18. If a business name includes a contraction (such as *don't* or *it's*), how should   18._____
    that word be treated in an alphabetical system?
    A. Divide the word into its separate parts and treat it as two words
    B. Ignore the letters that come after the apostrophe
    C. Ignore the word that contains the contraction
    D. Ignore the apostrophe and consider all letters in the contraction

19. In what order should the parts of an address be considered when using an alphabetical filing system?
    A. City or town; state; street name; house or building number
    B. State; city or town; street name; house or building number
    C. House or building number; street name; city or town; state
    D. Street name; city or town; state

20. A business record should be cross-referenced when a(n)
    A. organization is known by an abbreviated name
    B. business has a name change because of a sale, incorporation, or other reason
    C. business is known by a *coined* or common name which differs from a dictionary spelling
    D. all of the above

21. A geographical filing system is MOST effective when
    A. location is more important than name
    B. many names or titles sound alike
    C. dealing with companies who have offices all over the world
    D. filing personal and business files

Questions 22-25.

DIRECTIONS: Questions 22 through 25 are to be answered on the basis of the list of items below, which are to be filed geographically. Organize the items geographically and then answer the questions.

  I. University Press at Berkeley, U.S.
  II. Maria Sanchez, Mexico City, Mexico
  III. Great Expectations Ltd. in London, England
  IV. Justice League, Cape Town, South Africa, Africa
  V. Crown Pearls Ltd. in London, England
  VI. Joseph Prasad in London, England

22. Which of the following arrangements of the items is composed according to the policy of: *Continent, Country, City, Firm or Individual Name*?
    A. V, III, IV, VI, II, I   B. IV, V, III, VI, II, I
    C. I, IV, V, III, VI, II   D. IV, V, III, VI, I, II

23. Which of the following files is arranged according to the policy of: *Continent, Country, City, Firm or Individual Name*?
    A. South Africa; Africa; Cape Town; Justice League
    B. Mexico; Mexico City; Maria Sanchez
    C. North America; United States; Berkeley; University Press
    D. England; Europe; London; Prasad, Joseph

5 (#1)

24. Which of the following arrangements of the items is composed according to the policy of: *Country, City, Firm or Individual Name*?
    A. V, VI, III, II, IV, I
    B. I, V, VI, III, II, IV
    C. VI, V, III, II, IV, I
    D. V, III, VI, II, IV, I

25. Which of the following files is arranged according to a policy of: *Country, City, Firm or Individual Name*?
    A. England; London; Crown Pearls Ltd.
    B. North America; United States; Berkeley; University Press
    C. Africa; Cape Town; Justice League
    D. Mexico City; Mexico; Maria Sanchez

26. Under which of the following circumstances would a phonetic filing system be MOST effective?
    A. When the person in charge of filing can't spell very well
    B. With large files with names that sound alike
    C. With large files with names that are spelled alike
    D. All of the above

Questions 27-29.

DIRECTIONS: Questions 27 through 29 are to be answered on the basis of the following list of numerical files.

    I.   391-023-100
    II. 361-132-170
    III. 385-732-200
    IV. 381-432-150
    V.   391-632-387
    VI. 361-423-303
    VII. 391-123-271

27. Which of the following arrangements of the files follows a consecutive-digit system?
    A. II, III, IV, I   B. I, V, VII, III   C. II, IV, III, I   D. III, I, V, VII

28. Which of the following arrangements follows a terminal-digit system?
    A. I, VII, II, IV, III
    B. II, I, IV, V, VII
    C. VII, VI, V, IV, III
    D. I, IV, II, III, VII

29. Which of the following lists follows a middle-digit system?
    A. I, VII, II, VI, IV, V, III
    B. I, II, VII, IV, VI, V, III
    C. VII, II, I, III, V, VI, IV
    D. VII, I, II, IV, VI, V, III

Questions 30-31.

DIRECTIONS: Questions 30 and 31 are to be answered on the basis of the following information.

I. Reconfirm Laura Bates appointment with James Caldecort on December 12 at 9:30 A.M.
II. Laurence Kinder contact Julia Lucas on August 3 and set up a meeting for week of September 23 at 4 P.M.
III. John Lutz contact Larry Waverly on August 3 and set up appointment for September 23 at 9:30 A.M.
IV. Call for tickets for Gerry Stanton August 21 for New Jersey on September 23, flight 143 at 4:43 P.M.

30. A chronological file for the above information would be
    A. IV, III, II, I   B. III, II, IV, I   C. IV, II, III, I   D. III, I, II, IV

31. Using the above information, a chronological file for the date September 23 would be
    A. II, III, IV   B. III, I, IV   C. III, II, IV   D. IV, III, II

Questions 32-34.

DIRECTIONS: Questions 32 through 34 are to be answered on the basis of the following information.

I. Call Roger Epstein, Ashoke Naipaul, Jon Anderson, and Sara Washingon on April 19 at 1:00 P.M. to set up meeting with Alika D'Ornay for June 6 in New York.
II. Call Martin Ames before noon on April 19 to confirm afternoon meeting with Bob Greenwood on April 20th.
III. Set up meeting room at noon for 2:30 P.M. meeting on April 19th.
IV. Ashley Stanton contact Bob Greenwood at 9:00 A.M. on April 20 and set up meeting for June 6 at 8:30 A.M.
V. Carol Guiland contact Shelby Van Ness during afternoon of April 20 and set up meeting for June 6 at 10:00 A.M.
VI. Call airline and reserve tickets on June 6 for Roger Epstein trip to Denver on July 8.
VII. Meeting at 2:30 P.M. on April 19th.

32. A chronological file for all of the above information would be
    A. II, I, III, VII, V, IV, VI
    B. III, VII, II, I, IV, V, VI
    C. III, VII, I, II, V, IV, VI
    D. II, III, I, VII, IV, V, VI

33. A chronological file for the date of April 19th would be
    A. II, III, VII, I   B. II, III, I, VII   C. VII, I, III, II   D. III, VII, I, II

34. Add the following information to the file, and then create a chronological file for April 20th: VIII. April 20: 3:00 P.M. meeting between Bob Greenwood and Martin Ames. 34.____
   A. IV, V, VIII B. IV, VIII, V C. VIII, V, IV D. V, IV, VIII

35. The PRIMARY advantage of computer records over a manual system is 35.____
   A. speed of retrieval B. accuracy
   C. cost D. potential file loss

KEY (CORRECT ANSWERS)

1.	B	11.	D	21.	A	31.	C
2.	C	12.	C	22.	B	32.	D
3.	D	13.	B	23.	C	33.	B
4.	A	14.	C	24.	D	34.	A
5.	D	15.	D	25.	A	35.	A
6.	C	16.	B	26.	B		
7.	B	17.	C	27.	C		
8.	B	18.	D	28.	D		
9.	C	19.	A	29.	A		
10.	D	20.	D	30.	B		